NEW CENTURY BIBLE COMMENTARY

General Editors

RONALD E. CLEMENTS   MATTHEW BLACK
(Old Testament)   (New Testament)

Joel and Amos

THE NEW CENTURY BIBLE COMMENTARIES

EXODUS (J.P. Hyatt)
LEVITICUS (Philip J. Budd)
NUMBERS (Eryl Davies)
DEUTERONOMY (A.D.H. Mayes)
JOSHUA, JUDGES, RUTH (John Gray)
1 AND 2 KINGS, Volume 1 and 2 (Gwilym H. Jones)
1 AND 2 CHRONICLES (H.G. Williamson)
EZRA, NEHEMIAH AND ESTHER (D.J. Clines)
JOB (H.H. Rowley)
PSALMS, Volumes 1 and 2 (A.A. Anderson)
PROVERBS (R.N. Whybray)
ECCLESIASTES (R.N. Whybray)
THE SONG OF SONGS (John G. Snaith)
ISAIAH 1–39 (R.E. Clements)
ISAIAH 40–66 (R.N. Whybray)
JEREMIAH (Douglas Rawlinson Jones)
LAMENTATIONS (Iain Provan)
EZEKIEL (John W. Wevers)
HOSEA (G.I. Davies)
HAGGAI, ZECHARIAH AND MALACHI (Paul L. Redditt)
THE GOSPEL OF MATTHEW (David Hill)
THE GOSPEL OF MARK (Hugh Anderson)
THE GOSPEL OF LUKE (E. Earle Ellis)
THE GOSPEL OF JOHN (Barnabas Linders)
THE ACTS OF THE APOSTLES (William Neil)
ROMANS, Second Edition (Matthew Black)
1 AND 2 CORINTHIANS (F.F. Bruce)
GALATIANS (Donald Guthrie)
EPHESIANS (C. Leslie Mitton)
PHILIPPIANS (Ralph P. Martin)
COLOSSIANS AND PHILEMON (Ralph P. Martin)
1 AND 2 THESSALONIANS (I. Howard Marshall)
PASTORAL EPISTLES (A.T. Hanson)
HEBREWS (R. McL. Wilson)
1 PETER (Ernest Best)
JAMES, JUDE AND 2 PETER (E.M. Sidebottom)
JOHANNINE EPISTLES (K. Grayson)
THE BOOK OF REVELATION (G.R. Beasley-Murray)

Other titles are in preparation

NEW CENTURY BIBLE
COMMENTARY

JOEL AND AMOS

RICHARD JAMES COGGINS

Copyright © 2000 Sheffield Academic Press

Published by
Sheffield Academic Press Ltd
Mansion House
19 Kingfield Road
Sheffield S11 9AS
England

Typeset by Sheffield Academic Press
and
Printed on acid-free paper in Great Britain
by Cromwell Press
Trowbridge, Wiltshire

British Library Cataloguing in Publication Data

A catalogue record for this book is available
from the British Library

ISBN 1-84127-095-4

CONTENTS

PREFACE

The provision of a commentary on the Minor Prophets in the New Century Bible has gone through a number of vicissitudes. It was first envisaged that they would be dealt with as a whole. When it became apparent that this would not be feasible, the General Editor, Ronald Clements, did me the honour of asking me to contribute the commentary on Joel and Amos. Then it appeared that the whole project might be abandoned when a change of publishers became necessary, and the early stages of my own work had to be set aside. Eventually Sheffield Academic Press took over the series, and now, somewhat to my own surprise, I find myself with a manuscript which will I hope soon reach publication.

My first aim has been to provide a readable commentary. Many commentaries seem in recent years to have suffered a kind of elephantiasis, providing so much detailed information that it becomes almost impossible to follow the thread, either of the biblical text, or of the commentator's own thought. What follows aims to be readable, even if it will be charged with being superficial.

I owe especial thanks to Ronald Clements: for his determination in ensuring that the series did not fade out, for his invitation to me to contribute to the series, and for his forbearance when it became clear that our views, especially on Amos, do not wholly coincide. With regard to Joel I am particularly grateful to the Advanced Hebrew class at the Vacation Term for Biblical Study in Oxford, with whom I first studied that text in detail, and to Geoffrey Woods, who worked with me on Joel for his Master's degree. Study-groups, too numerous to list here, and of varying levels of academic expertise, have helped me to engage with Amos. They did not always agree with me, but the questions they asked provided an important stimulus, and their courtesy was always a model.

Richard Coggins
Lymington
November 1999.

ABBREVIATIONS

AB	Anchor Bible
ABD	David Noel Freedman (ed.), *The Anchor Bible Dictionary* (New York: Doubleday, 1992)
ATLA	American Theological Library Association
AV	Authorized Version
BDB	Francis Brown, S.R. Driver and Charles A Briggs, *A Hebrew and English Lexicon of the Old Testament* (Oxford: Clarendon Press, 1907)
BibInt	*Biblical Interpretation: A Journal of Contemporary Approaches*
BEATAJ	Beiträge zur Erforschung des Alten Testaments und des antiken Judentums
BKAT	Biblischer Kommentar: Altes Testament
BZAW	Beihefte zur ZAW
CBC	Cambridge Bible Commentary
CBQ	*Catholic Biblical Quarterly*
DCH	D.J.A. Clines (ed.), *Dictionary of Classical Hebrew* (Sheffield: Sheffield Academic Press, 1993–)
ICC	International Critical Commentary
Int	*Interpretation*
ISBE	Geoffrey Bromiley (ed.), *The International Standard Bible Encyclopedia* (4 vols.; Grand Rapids: Eerdmans, rev. edn, 1979–88)
JB	*Jerusalem Bible*
JBL	*Journal of Biblical Literature*
JSOT	*Journal for the Study of the Old Testament*
JSOTSup	*Journal for the Study of the Old Testament*, Supplement Series
JTS	*Journal of Theological Studies*
KAT	Kommentar zum Alten Testament
NEB	*New English Bible*
NRSV	New Revised Standard Version
OBO	Orbis biblicus et orientalis
OTG	Old Testament Guides
OTL	Old Testament Library
OTS	*Oudtestamentische Studiën*
REB	Revised English Bible
RSV	Revised Standard Version
RV	Revised Version

SBLDS	SBL Dissertation Series
SOTSMS	Society for Old Testament Study Monograph Series
TOTC	Tyndale Old Testament Commentaries
VT	*Vetus Testamentum*
VTSup	*Vetus Testamentum*, Supplements
ZAW	*Zeitschrift für die alttestamentliche Wissenschaft*

BIBLIOGRAPHY TO INTRODUCTION

Alter, R., and F. Kermode (ed.)
  1987   *The Literary Guide to the Bible* (London: Collins).
Barton, J.   *Oracles of God: Perceptions of Ancient Prophecy in Israel after the Exile*
            (London: Darton, Longman and Todd).
Brockington, L.H.
  1973   *The Hebrew Text of the Old Testament* (Oxford: Oxford University
            Press).
Carroll, R.P.
  1997   'Clio and Canons: In Search of a Cultural Poetics of the Hebrew Bible',
            BibInt 5.4 (1997): 300-23.
Coggins, R.J.
  1994   'The Minor Prophets—One Book or Twelve?', in S.E. Porter, P. Joyce
            and D.E. Orton (eds.), *Crossing the Boundaries: Essays in Biblical
            Interpretation in Honour of Michael D. Goulder* (Biblical Interpretation
            Series, 8; Leiden: E.J. Brill): 57-68.
  1996   'Interbiblical Quotations in Joel', in J. Barton and D.J. Reimer (eds.),
            After the Exile: Essays in Honour of Rex Mason (Macon, GA: Mercer
            University Press): 75-84.
Coote, R.B.
  1981   *Amos among the Prophets: Composition and Theology* (Philadelphia:
            Fortress Press).
Lemche, N.P.
  1998   *The Israelites in History and Tradition* (Library of Ancient Israel;
            London: SPCK).
Marks, H.
  1987   'The Twelve Prophets', in Alter and Kermode (eds.), 1987: 207-33.
Nogalski, J.
  1993a   *Literary Precursors to the Book of the Twelve* (BZAW, 217; Berlin: W.
            de Gruyter).
  1993b   *Redactional Processes in the Book of the Twelve* (BZAW, 218; Berlin:
            W. de Gruyter).
Swete, H.B
  1914   *Introduction to the Old Testament in Greek* (Cambridge: Cambridge
            University Press).
Thompson, T.L
  1999   *The Bible in History: How Writers Create a Past* (London: Jonathan
            Cape).

Watts, J.W., and P.R. House
    1996   *Forming Prophetic Literature: Essays on Isaiah and the Twelve in Honor
                of John D.W. Watts* (JSOTSup, 235; Sheffield: Academic Press, 1996).
Wolfe, R.E.
    1935   'The Editing of the Book of the Twelve', *ZAW* 53 (1935): 90-129.

INTRODUCTION

To write a commentary which is confined to chs. 2 and 3 of a book with 12 chapters would seem to be a curious undertaking; yet that could be one description of what is being attempted here. The section of the Hebrew Bible with which we are concerned is the 'Latter Prophets'. That section has four components: Isaiah, Jeremiah, Ezekiel and 'the Twelve'. These four are all of roughly comparable length; each has traditionally been regarded as a book in its own right.

Yet during the last three or four centuries, particularly in study of the material by scholars from a Christian tradition, the unity of the last book, the Twelve, has been almost completely neglected. Instead, its individual elements, usually described as 'the Minor Prophets', have been treated as distinct 'books' rather than as parts of one larger book. The normal conventions both of technical scholarship and of popular perception have led them to be regarded as twelve quite separate pieces of literature. Their different styles and different times and places of origin have led to the assumption that the individual books have nothing directly to do with one another. The only partial exception to this has been that Haggai and Zechariah 1–8 have commonly been treated together. Even these books have no cross-reference from one collection to the other; they are only referred to together outside their own books: Ezra 5.1; 6.14. But their juxtaposition within the Twelve, together with similarity of date and editorial structure, has invited this bracketing.

In other cases, however, the assumption has usually been made that the modern reader should approach the different units as separate books, and read them in the light of their supposed historical background. Thus Amos, Hosea and Micah have become 'the eighth-century prophets', Nahum, Habakkuk and Zephaniah have been placed, somewhat less confidently, in the seventh century, and Haggai, Zechariah and Malachi have been set in 'postexilic' times, the sixth and fifth centuries. These groupings have taken place, even though there is no cross-reference by any one prophet to any other. That is to say, on this reading Amos and Hosea must have been near contemporaries, each active in the same small area, but neither refers to the other. This is a point to which we must return when we look at Amos. With regard to the remaining collections, Joel, Obadiah and Jonah, there has been less confidence and more disagreement about dating, but in virtually every commentary on those books, too, the question of date is one of the first to be raised.

This kind of approach to the prophets has, however, come under scrutiny in recent years for a variety of reasons. We may notice four.

1. There is an obvious practical point which is often overlooked. It is difficult to envisage that twelve separate scrolls were preserved quite independently of one another, prior to their being brought together as one collection. This can never be more than an argument from silence, for we have no certain knowledge of the way in which any of what came to be the biblical material reached its final form.

2. An increasing interest in the history of interpretation has taken note of the fact that early understanding of these 'Minor Prophets' regularly saw them collectively, as 'the Twelve', rather than as an assorted group of individuals (Coggins 1994: 57-67). An outline of different explanations for the inter-relation of the Twelve is offered by Nogalski (1993a: 2-12), before he sets out his own proposals.

3. In many cases, a significant amount of secondary editing or redaction has been detected. The last few verses of Amos (Amos 9.8b, 11-15) provide a classic example of this. If the historical setting is to be regarded as of paramount importance then such later additions will be dismissed as 'secondary', with clear implications of inferiority. But if the whole book of Amos is to be treated seriously we must recognize it as a book with a happy, or at the very least a hopeful, ending, not simply as a collection of the dire threats which so dominate its main body. If these were later additions, Amos can no longer simply be regarded as an eighth-century collection, even if it remains probable (though by no means certain, as we shall see later) that the individual for whom it is named lived at that time. Such a different reading of Amos is bound to affect our consideration of Amos's place within the Twelve as a collection.

4. This last perception ties up with a different perspective in the reading of the other prophetic books, Isaiah, Jeremiah and Ezekiel. It has long been acknowledged that all 66 chapters of Isaiah can scarcely go back to the prophet himself, for they mention a character, Cyrus king of Persia, who lived 200 years after the apparent lifetime of Isaiah. To resolve this problem, 'extra' prophets were invented, and given the

names 'Deutero-' and 'Trito-Isaiah'. That may have preserved historical plausibility, but it did so at the expense of any perception of the unity of the whole Isaiah tradition. Recent studies of Jeremiah have also shown how tenuous is the connection between much of the material in the book and any historical figure of Jeremiah. Ezekiel has attracted less attention, but there too the complicated process by which the book reached its present form has come to be recognized.

When we look at the 'Book of the Twelve' it is obvious that it is even more varied than any of these other collections which make up the 'Latter Prophets'. Nevertheless, there is also an important sense in which we should perceive the Book of the Twelve as a unity. Its first main part (effectively from Hosea to Micah) is largely given over to threats, just as we find also in the early chapters of Isaiah, Jeremiah and Ezekiel, though here, as in those other books, hopeful passages may also be found. Oracles directed against foreign nations follow in the middle of all the collections; in Jeremiah, very briefly in the Hebrew form of the book, more extensively in its LXX form, widely regarded as more original. In the case of the Twelve these are found in Nahum, Habakkuk and Zephaniah 1–2. Again, as Isaiah, Jeremiah (again more obviously in LXX) and Ezekiel end on a more confident note, so it is in the Twelve, with the hopes embodied in Haggai, Zechariah and Malachi. It is recognized that there are anomalies in this outline picture; we can detect broad structures, while admitting that it is not always possible to detect why any of the collections have been built up in precisely the way they have. (I have looked at this phenomenon in slightly more detail in Coggins 1994: 64-67.)

Even in the two 'chapters' of the Book of the Twelve with which we have to deal, we shall notice some links which bind those chapters together. Some of these will be discussed in the commentary, but for the moment it is sufficient to notice the identity between parts of Joel 4.16 (MT 3.16) and Amos 1.2. There are comparable linkages between the end of Amos, especially 9.12, which speaks of 'the remnant of Edom', and the following book, Obadiah, which is similarly concerned with the inevitable destruction of Edom, but is not part of this commentary.

Reference has been made to Joel and Amos as comprising chs. 2 and 3 of the Book of the Twelve. That is true in the Hebrew tradition, the Masoretic Text, with which we shall primarily be concerned in this commentary. It should be borne in mind, however, that different orders have been preserved. In the main Greek (LXX) tradition, for example, represented by Codices Alexandrinus and Vaticanus, the order of the first six Minor Prophets is Hosea, Amos, Micah, Joel, Obadiah, Jonah (Swete 1914: 201-14). This is the order of the books in the standard edition of the LXX by Rahlfs 1949. In a comparable way, as we have already noted in looking at the outline structure of the different books, the Greek tradition preserves a different order within the book of Jeremiah, which many recent studies have tended to favour over against the Hebrew tradition. It is generally assumed that in the Twelve the Greek represents a secondary modification of the order, but this is an assumption rather than something which can be demonstrated. At the very least we are reminded that when we speak of the 'Book of the Twelve' the chapters do not necessarily follow one another in the way that would be required of a biography or a novel; there is something of an anthological principle at work also (so Marks 1987: 207).

This then raises another issue. Even the most cursory reading will show that it gives quite a misleading impression simply to regard Joel and Amos as no more than two chapters in one book. Though there are linkages, there are also radical differences: in style, in contents, in basic concerns. The question is thus raised whether the different elements of the Twelve simply represent a series of quite independent pieces which were brought together, if not by accident, then at least by a random, almost fortuitous process of growth, or are the result of a conscious structuring: what Dines has characterized as 'Argument from Accident' or 'Argument from Design'.[1] She notes that one of the points characteristically put forward in support of an argument from design is the fact of there being twelve Minor Prophets. Whatever the twelve may stand for (twelve patriarchs? twelve tribes? twelve judges?) it does not look like a random number. Nevertheless it should be borne in mind that some scholars have been much more doubtful whether anything of significance can be read into the order, or perhaps even the number, of the Minor Prophets (Barton 1986: 85).

We should also notice at this stage, though it is scarcely possible to explore the point in detail, that attempts have been made to work out in

---

1. J.M. Dines, 'The Unity of the Twelve: Approaches Old and New', p. 1. I am grateful to Dr Dines for letting me have a copy of her, as yet unpublished, paper. I very much hope that her paper will become more widely available, not least because of her perceptive comments on patristic commentaries on the Minor Prophets.

a more precise way the nature of the redactional process which has brought the Twelve together. As long ago as 1935 R.E. Wolfe proposed 13 distinct editorial stages through which the material had been brought so as to form the present collection (Wolfe 1935: 90-129). Wolfe wrote at a time when source-criticism was in its heyday, and was regarded as the most appropriate instrument to solve many problems of biblical study. Nogalski's work is less tied to source-critical assumptions. He traces two distinct literary corpora, one consisting of Hosea, Amos, Micah and Zephaniah, the other being Haggai and Zechariah 1–8. To these were added a 'Joel-related layer', incorporating elements from the remaining books of the twelve. I have tried elsewhere to point out some limitations in this approach (Coggins 1996: 75-84), but Nogalski's work is an essential starting-point for those concerned with the issue of the unity of the Twelve Minor Prophets (Nogalski 1993a and b). For those who wish to be introduced to the current debate two successive contributions to the Festschrift in honour of J.D. Watts (Watts and House 1996) may be noted. In the first, Nogalski, 'Intertextuality in the Twelve' summarizes the arguments from his two larger books, with particular reference to Joel; in the second E. Ben Zvi, 'Twelve Prophetic Books or "The Twelve": a Few Preliminary Considerations', expresses great scepticism as to a unified 'twelve', and argues in favour of twelve distinct collections, making Obadiah the starting-point of his arguments. In the detailed commentary we shall try to keep these issues under consideration, always bearing in mind the fact that the great majority of earlier commentaries from all theological standpoints have tended to treat the individual components of the Twelve very much as separate books.

One other consideration in the bringing together of the Twelve should be noted. We may assume that the juxtaposition of material which was in many ways so disparate was regarded as the making of a 'canon', the collective authority of which would override any inherent tensions. The group responsible for such shaping of the material, and the circumstances in which it took place, remain unknown to us, but we need not doubt that there were ideological factors involved. (See Carroll 1997: 315-21, for reflection on some of the implications of canon-making.)

We should notice in concluding this section that Joel has played a particular part in the proposed reconstruction of a 'Book of the Twelve' as a conscious unit, particularly because the number of allusions to and cross-references with other prophetic collections is perhaps greater in Joel than in any of the other components of 'the Twelve'. As already noted, Nogalski has made much of this in his two detailed studies of the 'Joel layer', and this is a point we shall need to bear in mind as we look at Joel in greater detail.

DATE

I shall look in more detail at the issue of dating in the introductions to Joel and Amos, but a general comment seems appropriate here. The standard view, as noted already, has regarded Joel and Amos as originating from very different periods. Amos, by almost universal consent, has been included among the 'eighth-century prophets', perhaps regarded as *the* archetypical eighth-century prophet. On the conventional reading of Israel's history, that is to say, he was active at a time when the Northern kingdom of Israel was enjoying a final brief period of prosperity before the rise of Assyria brought its dramatic end. The dating of Joel has been more disputed, but the great majority of scholars have placed it sometime in the 'postexilic' period. Despite attempts to be more precise, however, there is also strong agreement that no exact synchronisms are possible with Joel.

The outline of much of Israel's history, to which reference has just been made, is seen in many books with the title 'History of Israel' or the like. It consists essentially of a retelling of the biblical material. Such an approach has come under very close critical scrutiny in recent years. The implications of this reappraisal for our understanding of the prophetic books have not to my knowledge been worked out in detail as yet, but they must be very considerable. We shall see in the commentary on Amos that even in the book itself there are very few elements which specifically require an eighth-century setting. The well known account of the clash between Amos and Amaziah in 7.9-17 can certainly be taken as a story typifying clashes between rival claims to authority rather than as reliable history; and after that is removed all that remains which posits an eighth-century dating is the introductory verse (1.1), which is almost universally regarded as an editorial addition.

The argument of various recent writers concerning the dating and historical background of much of the Hebrew Bible, therefore, is that we should look at the external evidence, any kind of material which shows knowledge of our texts or provides an appropriate context for them, and start from that point. (Proposals along these lines have been made by many scholars; among the most compelling arguments set out in this sense are those of Lemche 1998.) The first reference to a collection of 'the Twelve' is almost certainly Sir. 49.10, which speaks of 'the bones of the Twelve Prophets'. That offers a dating in the early second century BCE, by which time the material had probably been brought together into something resembling its present form. We may assume quite an extended earlier history for the individual components of the two books, along with an editorial stage as the material was put into its final shape, but greater precision is impossible.

Since the sketch just offered goes so much against the conventional dating, it seems proper to set out briefly the assumptions concerning date which underlie this commentary, even though lack of more precise evidence means that they can only be very tentative. It seems proper to regard Joel as essentially a product of the Second Temple period, and most likely the book can be regarded as native to Jerusalem. To what extent it is itself a product of the Jerusalem cult, and to what extent it is better seen as conscious literary reflection upon the practices of that cult and the varied literary traditions which were maintained there, is an issue which we must consider in the introduction to Joel.

With Amos it seems likely that the basis of the book may be found in traditional material of somewhat greater age, possibly from a time when Israel had its own king, though the lack of reference to kings other than in 7.9-17 makes this far from certain. It has been argued that the condemnation of sacrifice found in Amos 5.21-22, and in other prophetic collections attributed to the eighth century, was actually a theme 'central to the intellectual currents of Hellenism' (Thompson 1999: 69), with the implication that the book should be regarded as a product of roughly the third century BCE, but this, though a very interesting general observation, is difficult to back up in detail. The treatment of 'Israel' as a separate state seems largely to be a literary device to enable the editor to embody it in the series of oracles in chs. 1–2; elsewhere in the book 'Israel' occurs very frequently as a designation of the community bound together by the worship of its god Yahweh. Various proposals have been made to attempt to spell out the editorial development of the book more precisely (e.g. Coote 1981), but the lack of a clear outline history means that they must remain speculative and are more useful for the incidental insights they offer than for their large-scale proposals.

The origin of the main collection of oracles in Amos, therefore, must remain uncertain. It may be a Jerusalemite collection, since the inhabitants of Jerusalem are condemned only once (6.1), whereas the practices and sometimes the very existence of other places (Samaria, Bethel, Gilgal) finds frequent condemnation. As with much propaganda literature, however, both in the ancient and in the modern world, it is easier to see what it is against than what it is for, and it gives few clues to original dating. We are reminded that we know much less about the day-to-day events of life in ancient Israel than the outline histories would lead us to suppose. All we can say with fair confidence is that the Amos collection was brought together in Jerusalem (1.2), and that a conscious effort was made to integrate it with the picture of the people's past offered by 2 Kings. (Details of this process will be noted in the commentary.) Opinions may differ as to the existence of an individual named 'Amos'. The name has no obvious 'meaning'; the rabbinic suggestion that he was a 'stutterer' is ingenious but scarcely historical. It certainly seems unlikely that he was no more than a free creation of later editors, but we know nothing of his life-setting.

The implication of this is that when 'Joel' and 'Amos' are referred to in this commentary, the reference will normally be to books rather than individuals. I shall not be much concerned with trying to identify 'secondary additions' and the like. Even if additions have been made to an original nucleus, it is important to remember that they are not simply accretions, to be scraped away so that the 'real' book can be discovered; they change the very character of the book. Particularly with Amos, the hopeful ending provided by the last few verses transforms the book as a whole. We have access only to the two collections in their final form, and that is what demands our attention.

THE TEXT TO BE COMMENTED UPON

What is offered here is a commentary upon the Masoretic Hebrew text in its traditional form, normally as represented by the New Revised Standard Version (NRSV) of the English Bible. That is the translation here used unless specific reference to the contrary is made. In both Joel and Amos the Hebrew text seems generally to have been preserved in good order, so that it is not very often that major proposals for a textual emendation have to be made. This is in marked contrast with the first element in the Book of the Twelve, Hosea, where textual problems abound. By comparison, that is to say, the number of suggested textual

emendations in Joel and Amos is small, and those that have commanded significant support can be looked at in context rather than as
part of any large-scale pattern. The New English Bible set out a number
of emendations to the Masoretic Text, some but not all of which have
survived in the REB; they are listed in Brockington 1973, and the
majority of them are discussed at the appropriate point in the commentary. In Joel the Hebrew text is divided into four chapters, whereas the
English versions, following LXX, have three. Reference to those parts of
Joel where Hebrew and English differ will here be given in the form
Joel 2.28 (MT 3.1).

Portions of the text of both Joel and Amos have been discovered at
Qumran and at the nearby Wadi Murabba'at, but these are modest dis-
coveries, both in their extent and in their implications for the text; reference to them can again be confined to the commentary. Similarly, reference will from time to time be made to other forms in which this
material has been handed down, notably the Greek Septuagint (LXX),
but it needs to be stressed from the outset that the Greek form of the
material is a different book from its original. This is not simply a matter
of language; we have already noted that the main Greek tradition has
preserved the material in a different order. Furthermore, it was speaking
to a different audience, and needs to be treated as a literary work (or
part of a larger one) in its own right.

COMMENTARY
ON JOEL

JOEL

1. AUTHORSHIP

As we have seen already, historical-critical conventions have established the custom that questions concerning authorship and date are the first to be raised when we look at a prophetic collection. That is the proper way, it is supposed, for 'genuineness' (or its lack) to be established. Yet for Joel these questions seem inappropriate. First of all, nothing is known of the author save his name. Even that statement is a little misleading. There is a general problem with all the prophetic collections: how far are the individuals for whom they are named properly considered as 'authors'? More specifically with regard to Joel, the frequent use of first-person pronouns in the book might seem intended to convey to us that it is Joel himself who is the author, the one speaking God's message. We should at least be open to the possibility that this is simply a literary device. (Since we know nothing of Joel in any case, this issue is somewhat academic, reminiscent of the old quip that Homer was written not by Homer but by someone else of the same name.) It does, however, have one important consequence. When we are speaking of 'Joel' it can be taken for granted that the reference is to the book so named rather than to an individual. Greater care in differentiation will be needed in the second part of this volume, dealing with Amos, for the important distinction between the book of Amos and the individual figure of Amos has often been blurred.

Secondly, the underlying implications of authorship questions with regard to Joel are significantly different from those which have customarily been raised for Amos. The usual picture of Amos has been of a block of genuine material supplemented at a later date by additions and modifications. With Joel, though proposals have been made that some small sections should be seen as later additions, the main discussion has centred around the unity of the book. We shall look below (section 3 of this Introduction) at the suggestion that the book should be divided into two, with a break at either 2.18 or 2.28 (MT 3.1), but we need also to bear in mind the proposal that the final form of the book should be regarded as the product of a particular group within Jerusalem cultic circles rather than the work of a single 'author'. We shall look at the proposals of Redditt 1986 in this sense in section 4 of this Introduction, but it may be useful to bear in mind from the outset that Bergler (1988: 16-19), in his detailed survey of scholarship on this issue, discerns increasing disillusionment as to the likelihood of our being able to achieve an answer.

Nevertheless, though we are unable to establish any details concerning 'Joel's' identity, it is important to recognize that the book named for him seems certainly to have links with the Jerusalem temple, and also to be clearly prophetic in form. Whether 'Joel' himself was a 'cultic prophet', fulfilling a specific role in the temple cult, remains an unanswerable question, but certainly the book offers us a critique of the practices of the temple from within, in a manner significantly different from the attacks upon cultic practice that we shall encounter in Amos.

2. DATE

The situation with regard to dating is almost as unpromising. We may begin by recalling Crenshaw's view that 'endeavors to establish a historical context for a biblical book constitute exercises in futility' (Crenshaw 1995: 28). This certainly seems to be true of Joel. Despite his own warning, Crenshaw is ready to accept the majority view that it is to be dated in the Second Temple period. That mode of expression will be used here rather than the more common 'postexilic', on two grounds. The first, more general point, is that the term 'postexilic' is often used as if 'the exile' was a phenomenon which had a datable beginning and end, both probably in the sixth century BCE. There has been much debate on this whole topic, but it certainly seems likely that some leading citizens of Judah, including the king Jehoiachin, were deported to Babylon at the time of Nebuchadrezzar of Babylon, and this came to be represented in the biblical tradition as an experience which affected the whole community and could be described as 'exile' rather than as 'deportation'. 'Exile' implies return, and the early chapters of Ezra offer us a picture of a mass return from exile, under Cyrus of Persia, but the historical evidence for such a movement is very slight, so that it becomes quite inappropriate to envisage 'the exile' as a brief and clearly defined period in the people's experience. The expression 'postexilic', though convenient, may therefore be quite misleading.

The second, more specific, point is that there is no clear reference to the exile or its consequences in Joel. We need not doubt that the deportation of some of its leading citizens had a profound effect upon the community of Judah, but we should not go on to suppose that this was a dominant theme in all the thought, or even all the religious writing, of the later community. The book of Joel is certainly concerned with the relation between Judah and its neighbours; see especially ch. 3 (MT ch. 4). The references in vv. 2-3 to 'scattering (my people) among the nations' could certainly be taken as an allusion to an exile, but it seems dangerous to attempt to read specific historical references from poetic language of the kind found in that passage.We shall see at 3.1 (MT 4.1) that the older understanding of the expression *šub šᵉbut* in the sense of bringing the exile to an end is no longer tenable. Thus, where KJV had 'bring again the captivity of Judah and Jerusalem', NRSV, in common with other recent translations, has 'restore the fortunes...'

We ought, however, to consider some of the criteria that have been proposed for the dating of this book, because there have been many exceptions to the consensus view just mentioned. For those who wish to pursue the question of date in greater detail two useful surveys have been published: Thompson (1974: 453-64) and Allen (1976: 19-25). Little new evidence has been adduced since then to modify Allen's conclusions. He begins by quoting Calvin to the effect that 'as there is no certainty it is better to leave the time in which (Joel) taught undecided, and as we shall see, this is of no great importance'. We may note that one of the most recent assessments of the question still holds that 'the date of the book of Joel remains a mystery' (Mason 1994: 116). It is striking that in the Old Testament Guides series in which Mason's work appeared Joel was 'relegated' for consideration after all the other prophetic collections except Haggai-Malachi, and that two of the most recent Introductions (Schmidt 1995; Soggin 1989) place Joel with Jonah at the end of all the prophetic books.

These uncertainties should be borne in mind as we consider briefly some of the arguments proposed for different datings. Despite their limitations they may give us some insight into the way in which the book has been assessed more generally.

Many conservative scholars have supposed that the order of the component parts of the 'Book of the Twelve' is relevant to dating. Archer, for example, held that this combined with historical allusions and linguistic evidence to make 'a theory of post-exilic composition quite untenable'; he could not leave the subject without noting that 'it is fair (!) to say that the arguments for a late date are largely based on humanistic philosophical assumptions' (Archer 1985: 314). We have seen already in the general introduction that the larger unity of the Twelve Prophets should certainly be borne in mind, but we saw also that the order of the components varied in different traditions. By and large it is very doubtful whether it offers clues to the date of Joel. It should also be noted that other conservative scholars have not felt inhibited by assumptions of this kind; Hubbard 1989, for example, regards a sixth- to fifth-century date as most likely, and he clearly regards the reuse of other Hebrew Bible material as an important characteristic of Joel.

Other grounds for an early dating have been proposed. It has been argued that similarities between the language of Joel and that found in the Ugaritic texts from Ras Shamra suggest an early date (Bic 1960), but Kapelrud had already drawn attention to these similarities and did not regard it as a necessary conclusion that Joel was itself early, seeing the book as dependent not only on such ancient traditions as those found at Ras Shamra but also on important elements in the Hebrew prophetic tradition (Kapelrud 1948: 16-18, 179). Indeed the idea of 'dependence' here is one that needs to be used with caution. If we were to envisage direct borrowing from Ras Shamra material, then an early date would indeed merit serious consideration. But it is much more likely that we are dealing with similar ideas and motifs rather than any direct linkage. Indeed Loretz has detected links with Canaanite tradition, but still proposes a very late dating. He finds in Joel a confrontation with a Canaanite practice of 'rain magic' and rituals for bringing rain. He then subjects Joel to an elaborate colometric analysis which in his judgment demonstrates the likelihood of a late literary development (Loretz 1986: 20-43 for the colometric analysis; 162 concerning dating). Whatever weight one gives to individual arguments, it is clear that links with Ugaritic or later Canaanite practice do not provide automatic guidance concerning dating.

On quite different grounds Koch has proposed a seventh-century dating. He maintains that 'day of the Lord' language, so prominent in Joel, is much more frequently found in works commonly dated to the Assyrian and Babylonian periods (Amos, Isaiah, Zephaniah, Obadiah), and that this provides a sounder basis for dating than the alleged links between Joel and the apocalypses (Koch 1982: 159-61). The weakness with this view is that it pays insufficient attention to the rich intertextual allusions which are so characteristic of Joel.

A third possibility for dating would be offered to us if we were able to trace precise historical allusions within the book. We shall have to consider in the commentary whether the locust plague of chs. 1–2 is a reference to an actual event or should be given symbolic significance. But even if it is historical, such plagues were endemic and cannot be taken as a reliable guide to dating. Another proposal has been to detect a reference to an eclipse of the sun at 2.31 (MT 3.4), and to suggest that this might offer sufficient clues to enable us to date the book (Stephenson 1969: 224-29). This seems to be an interesting example of a scholar from a scientific background (Stephenson is a geophysicist) wishing to introduce such criteria in a more precise way than the literary form allows.

No more helpful as criteria for dating are the references to other cities and nations in ch. 3 (MT ch. 4). Tyre and Sidon in v. 4, and the other places mentioned in vv. 6-8, and Egypt and Edom at v. 19, all played an important part in Judah's life at different periods, and in any case it is certainly possible that these should be seen as literary allusions rather than as relating to specific contemporary historical events. We must conclude that the book does not offer any precise historical criteria for proposing a date.

One other point has been noted as a possible pointer to a Second Temple dating: the lack of reference to a king, of the kind found in the introductory verses to Hosea, Amos, Micah and Zephaniah. This would be no more than an argument from silence if used as a basis for dating, but it links in an interesting way with Nogalski's proposal of a 'Joel layer' in the development of the 'Book of the Twelve'. He regards it as axiomatic that Joel represented a comparatively late literary stage in the process, the four books which do refer to a king having formed the basis of the corpus. His study presumes 'the first half of the fourth century' as the most likely date (Nogalski 1993b: 1, 48-57), though his main concerns are literary rather than historical.

This does suggest where the most reliable pointer to dating seems likely to be found. It is in the fact that Joel almost certainly quotes from and alludes to other prophetic texts. This is an issue which will concern us frequently in this commentary; we can say at the outset that in the majority of cases it seems likely that Joel was quoting rather than being quoted, and must therefore be later than the other works concerned.

One other characteristic feature of Joel has been drawn upon in the attempt to date the book. It has long been noted that there are similarities between the language used in Joel and that said to be characteristic of 'apocalyptic', the assumption being that such links automatically imply a late date. If apocalyptic was indeed the child of prophecy, as used commonly to be maintained, then the presence of apocalyptic features in Joel would automatically imply a very late stage of prophecy.

Such an argument would always have represented an oversimplification. Part of the difficulty arises from the fact that while what Cook describes as features of apocalyptic genres such as 'determinism, use of ciphers, and an emphasis on the ideas of fire and blood' are present in Joel (Cook 1995: 171), other features characteristic of the apocalypses—heavenly journeys, the intervention of angels, overt animal symbolism—are lacking. This has led to a distinct ambivalence in scholarly attitudes on the question of the relation between Joel and the apocalypses. Crenshaw (1995: 25) may be taken as characteristic. He wishes to see in Joel 'a transition between prophecy and apocalyptic'. Certainly the argument that Joel's eschatological concerns enable us to trace a development, from Joel, through Zechariah 12–14 and Isaiah 24–27 to Daniel, with Joel on this basis dated in the fourth century (thus Plöger 1968: 96-105) would be regarded with great caution by most recent writers. Our knowledge of the Jerusalem community, its social structure and its literary activity, during the Persian period, is an inadequate basis for precise analysis.

3. UNITY

It has been widely argued that the book of Joel consists of two distinct units. Some have claimed that the break occurs at 2.18, but the more usual view has been to separate 1.1–2.27 from what follows. On this view the first half is more like other prophetic texts in being concerned with historical events, in this case a plague of locusts seen as the precursor of the day of Yahweh, whereas ch. 3 (MT chs. 3–4) deal with the day of Yahweh itself. This view comes from the time when source-critical analysis was primary in the scrutiny of biblical texts. Thus an older commentator such as Bewer (1912) began his study with a section entitled 'The Composition of the Book' in which he maintained, not so much that chs. 1–2 and 3–4 of MT had different origins, as that three different hands could be traced in the work. This kind of detailed analysis, never accepted by more conservative commentators, has fallen out of favour in more recent critical study. Partly there has been a crisis of

confidence: can we really claim the detailed knowledge of ancient literary habits which would allow such precise delineation of authors and
sources? Partly too, as we shall see below, there has been increased
recognition on both literary and theological grounds that our primary
concern must be with the text handed down to us.

The proposal that it is possible to distinguish between 'prophetic' and
'apocalyptic' elements in the book has also come to seem to be an
unsatisfactory basis for division. It is indeed the case that the imagery
of 2.28–3.21 (MT chs. 3–4) becomes more surreal, less rooted in day-to-
day living, but the links between different parts of the book warn
against breaking it up into distinct elements. There have been various
attempts to discern particular structures within the final form of the
book. Crenshaw (1995: 29-34) outlines a variety of such proposals, all
of them at odds with one another. (Since Crenshaw wrote another such
proposal has been made by Cook (1995: 184-85), who sets out a list
showing continuity between 2.1-11 and 2.28–3.21 [MT chs. 3–4]. It
seems best to regard such suggestions as a form of reader-response
criticism. If the discerning of a particular structure is of value in helping
a particular reader to achieve a better understanding of the book, then it
can be welcomed as such; it should not necessarily be regarded as having any objective status.

These uncertainties provide some of the background for the much
greater interest in the final form in which the book has come down to us
rather than in its pre-history, the stages by which that form was reached.
This interest arises from the concerns of what is sometimes called
'canonical criticism', paying attention to the way in which the book has
been seen as Scripture by the religious communities in which it was
handed down. Interestingly, the best-known proponent of this approach
distinguishes between the 'canonical shape' of Joel, which is certainly a
unity, and what he regards as probably a more complicated pre-history,
involving a redactional process (Childs 1979: 389). It is also possible
that Joel came to be esteemed in a way that we might describe as
regarding it as 'Scripture', without it being part of a formal canon. But
for this there is no evidence.

Interest in the final form of the book also arises from the influence of
general literary criticism, from which in the past biblical study was
often isolated. Literary critics normally pay much more attention to the
final form of a work than to the stages by which it may have reached
that form. Thus several recent commentators, not all of them particu-

larly conservative in their approach, have reacted against the division of
the book, and wish rather to stress its unity in the form in which it has
come down to us. That approach will be followed here.

4. WHAT KIND OF BOOK?

Even a surface reading of Joel soon shows us that we are concerned
with something different from the standard picture of a prophetic book.
The usual view, well-illustrated by Amos, Hosea and Micah, as well as
by the larger prophetic collections, is of a series of oracles against the
community, interspersed occasionally with words of reassurance, and
featuring also in some cases oracles against foreign nations. From collections such as these it has proved possible to build up an overall
image of 'the prophetic message'.

But it is virtually impossible to fit Joel neatly into a picture of that
kind. Some elements of it are indeed present: there is certainly condemnation of and attacks on various wrong practices, but these are rarely
specified in the way that we shall find to be characteristic in the latter
part of this volume when we look at Amos. In addition the form in
which these condemnations are delivered differs markedly from what
we find in what have come to be regarded as the mainstream prophets.
Thus the theme of 'the day of Yahweh' is prominent in both Joel and
Amos, and in each case is regarded as an ominous occasion, a profound
threat to the community's well-being. Yet its presentation is very different, as may be seen by comparing Joel 1.15 with Amos 5.18. It is this
difference, together with the absence of any reliable criteria for dating,
that has been one factor in suggesting a Second Temple dating for Joel,
with the implication that the circumstances of the community had
changed very drastically. In any case, as we have already seen, it is
clear that any proposals concerning the background of the book of Joel
must be very tentative. Broadly speaking two lines of argument have
been maintained with regard to the classification of Joel. Each has its
strengths, though it is unlikely that both can be wholly right.

5. A CULTIC CONTEXT?

It may be relevant here to note that the last 50 years or so of scholarly
debate have seen much discussion of 'cultic prophets'. An older view
cited familiar verses from Amos (5.21-24), and other prophets to maintain that the prophets were radically opposed to the cult. Such a view is

scarcely appropriate for Amos, as we shall see later in this volume, but
it is clearly inappropriate for some of the other components of the
'Book of the Twelve', including Joel. It has therefore been widely
maintained that there were 'cultic prophets', perhaps in the First
Temple, more certainly in the Second Temple, and that possibly Joel as
an individual, and certainly the book that bears his name, may be seen
as an example of this cultic prophecy. (I have attempted in an earlier
essay to assess the evidence for this 'alternative prophetic tradition'
[Coggins 1982]).

This provides the context for the first of the two readings of Joel
mentioned above. In it the locust plague, taken to be a historical event
rather than (or at least, as well as) a literary device, is seen as the occasion for national laments and we thus gain some insight into the
Jerusalem temple cult. Most probably, as we have seen, this is the cult
of the Second Temple, traditionally said to have been completed in the
late sixth century BCE, though the pre-exilic temple is also a possibility.
This understanding of Joel was put forward by Kapelrud (1948), though
he maintained a First Temple dating, and developed by, among other
scholars, Ahlstrom (1971), and by Redditt (1986), whose article offers a
useful approach into some recent discussion of the background of Joel.

In his view the book offers us insights into disputes within the
Second Temple community at Jerusalem. The early part of the book
shows attacks on the priesthood for allowing the pattern of daily
sacrifices to be interrupted. Such attacks had the effect of excluding the
group represented by the book from 'central' status within the cult.
They were reduced to 'peripheral' status. Redditt uses this approach to
account for differences within the book. As far as 2.17 Joel may be
regarded as 'central', and could address the priests directly. Later parts
of the book express views which in terms of the sociology of religion
can only be described as 'sectarian'. For example, prophecy is
democratized and a welcome is offered to a variety of charismatic gifts
in 2.28-32 (MT ch. 3). On this reading Redditt maintains that the group
represented by Joel was an heir to prophetic rather than priestly
traditions. This would certainly account for the extensive quotations
from the prophetic literature; on the other hand the assumption that a
prophetic group which felt itself to be under threat would welcome the
extension of prophetic status to all and sundry seems much more dubious. A useful outline of recent views of Joel's placing within a Second
Temple context is provided by Cook (1995: 168-71); his conclusion is

that Joel is 'a unity, an apocalyptic text produced by temple officials' (p. 171). He is also very sceptical of Redditt's claim to see antagonism toward the temple and its cult emerging within the book.

6. INTERTEXTUALITY IN JOEL

The quotations from other parts of Scripture to which reference has just been made provides the focus for the other approach which I must now consider. Here we are particularly concerned with inner-biblical exegesis, and especially the unusually large number of places where it looks as if Joel is commenting upon, sometimes elaborating, sometimes modifying, earlier prophetic material. We shall see examples of that as we work through the text, but it may be helpful here to set out the most generally accepted such passages. Mason (1994: 117-20) offers a useful brief summary of the most striking of these parallels, but we shall here follow the list offered by Williamson (*ISBE* II, 1078).

He lists 1.15 as reflecting Ezek. 30.2-3; Isa. 13.6 and Zeph. 1.7

    2.2–Zeph. 1.14f
    2.3 reverses Isa. 51.3; Ezek. 36.35
    2.6–Nah. 2.10
    2.17–Ps. 79.10
    2.27–Ezek. 36.11 (and frequently); Isa. 45.5-6, 18
    2.28 (MT 3.1)–Ezek. 39.29
    2.31 (MT 3.4)–Mal. 4.5 (MT 3.23)
    2.32 (MT 3.5)–Obad. 17
    3.4 (MT 4.4)–Obad. 15
    3.10 (MT 4.10) reverses Isa. 2.4; Mic. 4.3
    3.16 (MT 4.16)–Amos 1.2; Isa. 13.13
    3.17 (MT 4.17)–Ezek. 36.11
    3.18 (MT 4.18)–Amos 9.13

It is important also to note Williamson's following comment that 'many briefer parallels and allusions are also to be found'. We note straightaway that, with the single exception of Psalm 79, all the passages to which cross-references appear are from the Prophets.

This phenomenon has long been recognized. It was, for example, a major feature of the discussion in the commentary of Wolff (1977, especially pp. 10-12), but it has been given fresh impetus by recent scholarly interest in the whole phenomenon of intertextuality within the Hebrew Bible. (Curiously Fishbane 1985, which is often rightly referred to as the first major modern study in this field, makes very little reference to Joel.)

One of the difficulties that confronts a deeper understanding of this phenomenon is that the quotations and allusions depend purely on our recognition of them, and this at once introduces a subjective element: in any walk of life we all tend to see what we are looking for and expect to find. Thus Nogalski, concerned particularly to develop his theory of the development of the Book of the Twelve, scarcely refers to the links with other parts of the Hebrew Bible, but finds additional links between Joel and other parts of the Twelve, some of which we shall look at in a moment.

A comparison with New Testament usage may be helpful. It is well-known that within the New Testament it is not always clear whether a specific allusion is being made to a particular Old Testament text. At least in the New Testament the problem is sometimes eased when we find 'It is written' or some such expression, which we know will denote a reference to the Scriptures, our Hebrew Bible. Similarly the Dead Sea Scrolls commonly make it clear when they are engaged in the interpretation of biblical material. With Joel no such clues are afforded. It is possible that there may have been ' "stock" prophetic oracles which could be reused, and like sermon material today, put to different exegetical purposes' (Mason 1994: 119). Part of our difficulty arises from the fact that we have no means of being sure how widely known and recognized was the material which we have now come to accept as 'biblical'. Would the original hearers or readers of Joel have picked up the allusions that have been detected by modern scholars, often through the use of various forms of information technology? In some cases we may feel they may well have done so: the reversal of the 'swords into ploughshares' motif at 3.10 (MT 4.10) is an obvious case in point. Some of the other passages listed above, and in particular the 'briefer parallels and allusions', seem scarcely likely to have been recognized by those hearing them without previous warning.

All of this suggests a consciously learned, or didactic, purpose for Joel. It is markedly different from those approaches to the book that discern in it strong polemic against other religious groups. It does tie in with the approach set out by Nogalski, who has put forward a major proposal for understanding this phenomenon in the context of the Book of the Twelve (Nogalski 1993a and b). He sees in Joel part of a deliberate structuring as one stage of the process of forming the Book of the Twelve. To do this he goes significantly beyond the list of cross-references listed above, and not all of his suggestions will necessarily be accepted. Thus, he gives considerable weight to supposed links between the last verses of Hosea and Joel 1.1-14 (Nogalski 1993b: 13-14). In fact the five 'key words' which he there identifies as links are all very common ('this', 'inhabitants', 'wine', 'vine', 'grain'), and the two passages differ so greatly in other respects that it is doubtful whether ordinary readers of Hosea and Joel would have recognized any deliberate linkage (Coggins 1996: 77). There are other references within the Book of the Twelve, which he claims lend support to his proposal of 'Redactional Processes in the Book of the Twelve' (the title of Nogalski 1993b). Thus he finds linkages between Joel 1.12 and Hag. 2.19, between Joel 2.18 and Zech. 8.12, and between 3.1 (MT 4.1) and Zeph. 3.20, as well as a more elaborate pattern of cross-reference between Joel 2.1-2 and Zeph. 1.15-16 than that noted above (Nogalski 1993a: 301). We should note too that he either plays down or ignores the references to Isaiah and Ezekiel which are an equally striking feature of the list set out by Williamson.

Despite the reservations that we have expressed about some of the linkages that Nogalski claims to detect, it is undeniable that he has opened an important area for study, and we should certainly be alert for associations of this kind. As we work through the text, we shall need to consider whether a particular link seems better understood as part of a conscious editorial process or as the borrowing of a quotation or an allusion deemed appropriate for the occasion.

A more modest way of expressing this point is to speak of an 'anthological quality' (Crenshaw 1995: 36. As far as I am able to judge Crenshaw was aware of Nogalski's work, which is included in his bibliography, but was not able to subject it to detailed scrutiny: it is mentioned only in one footnote). Thus to express the matter leaves open the question whether we are dealing with specific allusions to written texts or with more general knowledge of tradition, which might have been handed down orally or within a cultic setting. From 'garden of Eden' language (2.3), through allusions to the plagues of Egypt and the Exodus, right on to the picture of an ideal future, the whole book is rich with cross-references to other aspects of the people's traditions. (Bergler 1988 explores this with a broader frame of reference than that of Nogalski; particularly striking are some of the links he establishes between Joel and the plague-traditions in Exodus.) When in addition we bear in mind the propensity for repetition found in Joel, we shall discover that there is scarcely a verse that does not evoke some other theme from within the Hebrew Bible. Such richness of allusion may be held to support a late date in the most general terms, but warns against any attempt at precision in dating.

We should be wise to admit that our knowledge is inadequate to come to a final decision whether the didactic approach which has just been outlined is more persuasive than the cultic and polemic context suggested earlier. My own feeling is that it would be unsafe to discount the latter element. I have been trying to explore the relation between these two elements since my first engagement with the book of Joel nearly 20 years ago (Coggins 1982: esp. 88-90), and the combination of cultic language with the denunciation of the way in which that cult was performed still seem to be dominant features of the book. Cook (1995: 209) ends his interesting discussion of the book by claiming that 'there is no evidence of polemic in Joel'. It is true that there are no direct denunciations of the kind characteristic of Amos, and indeed of other prophetic collections. But, as we shall see as we look at the text in more detail, there is much in Joel which can certainly be interpreted as expressing serious dissatisfaction with the cultic practice of its day.

7. TEXT AND VERSIONS

This commentary is based upon the Hebrew Masoretic Text, normally as translated in NRSV. The various fragments of Joel found at Qumran and Muraba'at do not raise major new issues for interpretation, and will only be mentioned in passing at the appropriate places. As already noted in the Introduction, the one point which calls for care in checking references is the fact that the Hebrew text divides the book into four chapters, whereas all English versions include ch. 3 of the Hebrew within ch. 2 (2.28-32). Chapter 4 of the Hebrew is thus ch. 3 in English versions. Within this commentary the English is normally quoted first with the Hebrew reference, where it differs, added in brackets.

COMMENTARY

1.1. The form of this verse is identical with the first part of the opening verses of Hosea, Micah and Zephaniah. In the other prophetic collections the comparable words are followed by a reference to the reigns of the kings under whom they were claimed to be active. Joel lacks any such cross-reference, which may imply either a Second Temple dating, when there were no native kings, or the early loss of knowledge of, or interest in, the date of Joel. What is to follow is '**the word** [sing.] **of the Lord**'. Presumably that is to be understood as a reference to the collection as a whole, rather than to a series of oracles which would be better described as 'word*s* of the Lord'. We shall note that Amos 1.1 contains no reference to the Lord; that book consists of Amos's own words, in whatever way we may understand their inspiration.

The name **Joel** is a common one in the Hebrew Bible, with at least twelve, and perhaps more (see *ABD* III: 872-73), characters so called, and there are no grounds for identifying our Joel with any of the others. The 'meaning' of the name is simple enough: 'Yah(weh) is God'; it is effectively the same name as 'Elijah', with the two elements reversed in order. But the word 'meaning' in the last sentence is deliberately put in inverted commas, for it is very doubtful whether any special significance should be seen in the name. At one time it was fashionable to suppose that the names borne by Old Testament characters somehow told us something about their inner lives, and the way they were perceived by others, but there is little evidence to support such a view.

By contrast with the frequency of the name Joel, that of his father **Pethuel** is found only here in the Hebrew Bible. In LXX and Syriac the form 'Bethuel' is found. This could be an error in transcription, but is more likely to be an example of the tendency in much biblical interpretation to link otherwise unknown characters with those about whom some information was available. 'Bethuel' is known as the father of Rebekah, the wife of the patriarch Isaac (Gen. 22.23; 24.47).

1.2-14. This section functions as an introduction to the main body of the book. There is dispute whether this introductory section should be confined to vv. 2-12, but vv. 13-14 are better seen as the climax of what has preceded rather than as a new start, not least because of links in vocabulary between vv. 2 and 14 (**elders...inhabitants of the lands**). Only very gradually does the picture that is being outlined become clear. As we shall see in a moment, the language of v. 2 implies that a crisis has taken place, but its nature is not at once revealed. If we assume that the locusts first mentioned in v. 4 are real, rather than themselves being a metaphor for more general disaster, then at that point the theme becomes more specific. The remainder of this section describes the disaster in a variety of pictures, but it is only at the next stage in the unfolding of the total scenario (v. 15) that we are made aware that all this is the LORD's doing, that it is indeed closely related to the 'day of the LORD'.

1.2. In one sense the message can be said to begin immediately, but in another sense we are still at a very preliminary stage. This and the next verse are in effect a 'summons to receive instruction' (Wolff 1977:20) rather than anything more specific. We are not yet told what the **such a thing** of this verse or the 'it' of v. 3 may be. Again we notice a formal link with Hosea, where in 5.1 it was the 'priests' and the 'house', both 'of Israel' and 'of the king' who were summoned. It is not necessary to suppose that **elders** refers to any formally recognized group within the community; they are simply the senior citizens, among whom the accumulated experience and wisdom of the community might legitimately be sought. Literally translated the Hebrew would be 'Hear this, the elders', but NRSV is surely right in seeing the article as being in effect a vocative: **Hear this, O elders**. Most commentators have assumed that **this** refers to the message that is to follow, but Nogalski 1993b: 15-16 argues that 'the most natural reading would expect that something had preceded the verse to which "this" now refers. Hos. 14.2ff provides the expected background.' This proposal ties in with Nogalski's argument, noted in the introduction, that the earlier verses of Joel form a conscious link with the end of Hosea, They also form part of his larger suggestion of a 'Joel-related layer' in the redaction of the Twelve Minor Prophets, with the implication that they should be read as one book rather than as twelve separate collections. (See the introduction above for a more general consideration of this point.)

Those addressed are clearly **the inhabitants of the land**, that is, Jerusalem and whatever surrounding area was linked with it in Joel's time, but the Greek tradition again shows how interpretation developed by supposing that it was the inhabitants of the whole world that were to be involved.

1.3. However great may be the disaster which Joel is about to describe, it will not involve the complete annihilation of the community. There will be **children** down to a fourth generation to learn of what has happened. It is possible, though not likely, that we should see here an allusion to God's purposes being carried through to the third and fourth generation in the Ten Commandments (Exod. 20.6). In any case there is no doubting the literary skill which builds up the tension; **it** is to be told to great-grandchildren, but we still do not know what 'it' is. A similar literary strategy underlies the opening verses of Psalm 78.

1.4. Now at last we are given an insight into the nature of the affliction. It is a devastating **locust** plague. It is certainly possible that the reference here is to an actual historical event. Locusts have plagued the whole of the Middle East down to our own century; the last very severe attack to have affected Jerusalem is said to have taken place in 1915. Even today pesticides are of limited use in repelling them. Yet precisely because of their devastating effect, references to locusts occur several times in the Hebrew Bible in a symbolic sense, as a metaphor of unstoppable destruction. Opinions will differ whether the locusts which formed one of the 'plagues of Egypt' (Exod. 10.4-19) were real or symbolic, but the latter sense is clear in such passages as Deut. 28.38, 1 Kgs 8.37 and Nah. 3.15-17. There is only one further specific reference to locusts in Joel (2.25, which forms a kind of inclusio with our present verse), and it may perhaps tentatively be suggested that the symbolic force is primary here.

However that may be, another problem arises with the reference to **cutting, swarming, hopping** and **destroying** creatures. It is possible that these names are used for four different kinds of locust; the English versions seem for the most part to assume that to be the case, particularly REB, which distinguishes between 'locust' and 'swarmer', 'hopper' and 'grub'. Another possibility is that the names denote different stages in the formation of the insect. But readings of this kind give the impression that our author's main concern was zoological, and that he wished to give precise analysis of the devastation and its causes. It seems much more likely that his intention was to use these different words as a vivid way of conveying the range and extent of the devastation whose immediate cause was pictured as locusts but whose real instigator was God.

Of the names used *gāzām*, NRSV 'cutting locust', is a term found only in its two occurrences in Joel (here and 2.25) and in Amos 4. 9, where it is simply translated 'locust' (as in REB here). We may possibly see in the present reference a deliberate allusion to Amos. Were this cross-reference to be the only one of its kind, its significance would be very slight, but we shall see that there are a number of such allusions in Joel, which collectively may have more weight.

By contrast the second term, *'arbeh*, is more widely used; this is the locust of the Exodus plague. Bergler 1988 sees this as an important element in his view of Joel as a reinterpretation of the Exodus theme and he devotes a specific section (pp. 256-58) to exploring the literary and thematic links. We should also notice that *'arbeh* is used as a symbol of great numbers (Judg. 7.12; Jer. 46.23). It can only be speculation, but one wonders whether the similar looking and sounding word *'arba'* used for 'four' and its multiples, had any effect in developing this sense of multitude.

The third term, *yeleq*, is used at Ps. 105.34 in parallel with *'arbeh* to describe the Egyptian locust plague (NRSV: 'young locusts'), and at Nah. 3.16, as part of the cry of vengeance against Nineveh, where the reference to locusts is found in parallel with fire and sword as symbolizing destruction. We probably need not concern ourselves too much with its characterization here as a 'hopping locust'; all locusts can be pictured as moving in that way.

Finally, 'the destroying locust', *ḥāsil*, introduces another term, again used in one of the descriptions of the plagues of Egypt found in the Psalms (Ps. 78.46), and as part of an extensive list of potential disasters ('plague, blight, mildew...') at 1 Kgs 8.37.

One other point about this verse merits attention. The theme of 'remnant' in the prophets has sometimes been given a hopeful sense, the point being emphasized that destruction, though severe, is not total (cf. Isa. 10.20-21). Though there will be children and grandchildren to be told about the disaster (v. 3), there is otherwise little of that sense even implied here: what is **left** by one plague is only allowed to survive so that another may come and destroy it.

1.5. What can be done about such devastation? It is too late for any effective action; the only recourse is lament. So we find a summons to lament. Whereas the opening summons to receive instruction had been addressed to 'all the inhabitants of the land', now it appears as if this summons is addressed to a more limited group, presumably the leaders of the community. But, as in Isa. 5.11-12, their leadership has only taken the form of outdoing others in drinking. The Hebrew Bible has many condemnations of **drunkards**, from Noah onwards (Gen. 9.21, though there the main condemnation is less of Noah himself than of his son Ham). As in Noah's case, drunkenness is commonly associated with sleep, and therefore an inability to discern the significance of what is going on.

So it is here. Those accused are to **wake up**. When they do so they will **weep** and **wail**. At first their laments will apparently only be because there is nothing more to drink; the **sweet wine** (*'āsis*) is to be, in a curious phrase, **cut off**. Why this kind of wine should be described as 'sweet' we do not know (in REB it is 'new wine'), but its use here and in a much more hopeful context in 3.18 (MT 4.18) provides another literary link with Amos (9.13). The verb *yalal*, 'wail' is probably onomatopoeic, and may well be chosen for its similar sound to, but profoundly different meaning from, *halal*, to praise.

1.6. The summons to lament, inviting a response like the community laments in the Psalms, is now developed. That we are confronted with metaphorical language is clear; less clear is the referent of the metaphor. The **nation... powerful and innumerable** no doubt refers to the locusts of v.4, and *'aṣum*, 'powerful', is a favourite word to describe them (cf. 2.2, 5). It may be that the vivid description that follows is simply an elaboration of the effect of that plague. But if the locusts are themselves symbolic of some other evil that has afflicted the community we have to confess that we cannot know the details. The difficulty may be simply expressed: there is much in the following verses that would make good sense as alluding to a locust plague, and that can be taken as the basis of the lament. But there is also much that seems less suited to such a reference, and we then have to decide whether we are still dealing with increasingly far-fetched descriptions of locusts, or whether the whole picture, locusts and all, is essentially symbolic of the evil facing a God-forsaken community.

The shift to first-person usage in this verse, as if Yahweh himself is now speaking, caused problems for those older commentators who were much concerned with source-analysis (Bewer 1912: 78), but is now generally accepted as a dramatic literary device. Joel is no longer merely speaking on behalf of Yahweh, but is actually uttering his words. Elsewhere Yahweh himself is likened to a lion. In Hos. 11.10; 13.8 the same two words, *'aryeh* and *lābi'*, here translated **lions'** and **lioness**, are used, though in Hosea 13 NRSV has 'lion' for *lābi'*. Those who have seen a deliberate linkage between Hosea and Joel can see part of the terror here as arising from the fact that whereas in Hosea Yahweh had acted as a lion on behalf of his people, now the lion is an alien power being allowed by Yahweh to terrorize his own followers. It is as if Yahweh himself is under threat from the enemy, for it is **my land** (and in v. 7 **my vines** and **my fig trees**) which are being attacked.

1.7. **Vines** and **fig trees** symbolized the ideal state of affairs, when (male) members of the community sat 'under their own vines and under their own fig trees' in peace and security (Mic. 4.4, a passage added at the end of the prophecy held in common with Isaiah of swords and spears becoming ploughshares and pruning hooks). The laying waste envisaged here may be a deliberate reversal of the Micah prophecy. Vines and fig trees are also referred to in Hos. 2.12 (MT 2.14), but the context there is somewhat different. The exact meaning of q^e*ṣāpāh* (NRSV 'splintered', REB 'broken', is uncertain: the word occurs in this form only here, though the same root is used to describe the fate of the king of Samaria in Hos. 10.7 ['like a chip']). One wonders, however, whether the much more common *q-ṣ-p* root, implying anger, may not be in the author's mind here. However that may be, this is one of several passages in Joel which owe much of their effect to alliteration, with the building up of sibilants and labials: *śām gapni l^{e}šammāh ut$^{e'}$enāti liq^{e}ṣāpāh ḥāśap ḥ^{a}śāpāh.*

The overall picture is clearly one of total devastation; the way in which it is described is certainly compatible with the effect of a locust plague. A slight emendation of the Hebrew of the last phrase has often been proposed (see BHS), to give a smoother translation, 'it has stripped it, throwing it down as it stripped'; but the main point is probably the overall poetic effect rather than precise accuracy in translation.

1.8. The meaning of the first word, '^{e}*li*, can only be deduced from the context. The common verb '*alah*, 'curse', is clearly inappropriate here; dictionaries have assumed the existence of a second verb, found only here, meaning 'mourn' or 'lament'. Its meaning was already obscure by the time of the Greek translation, for the LXX takes the word to be a preposition with suffix, 'to me' and renders the verse quite differently. Part of the problem arises from the fact that other comparable summonses in vv. 5, 11 and 13 indicate who is to take action; here no specific group is named. Wolff (1977: 18) conjectures that 'scribal mutilation' has taken place, and that v. 9b originally stood before v. 8. It is an attractive suggestion, but unsupported by any specific evidence, and Crenshaw (1995: 97) rightly warns against the tendency to 'correct' an unusual structure simply because it is found only in Joel.

The simile of the virgin dressed in sackcloth could be an allusion to

Jerusalem (cf. the frequent use of 'daughter Zion' language in Isaiah and elsewhere), but could equally stand on its own. An obvious difficulty arises from the description of a **virgin** having had a **husband**. Some have supposed that *bᵉtulāh* need not necessarily mean 'virgin', but simply any young woman, or that the 'husband' may be the man to whom she was betrothed without any implication that they were already man and wife. Perhaps enquiries of this kind are attempts to give too precise a reference to poetic language.

1.9. The cultic context of Joel emerges clearly for the first time in this verse, where the unavailability of the material for sacrifices, and the mourning of the temple ministrants, are stressed. Whether this is specifically the result of the locusts' devastation or a more general picture of dereliction is not made clear. Specific reference to **the grain offering and the drink offering** as part of the regular round of cultic requirements is found only in texts usually linked to the Second Temple period, and some scholars (e.g. Wolff) have seen this as a pointer to the date of Joel. But it is not a strong argument; though we know little of the worship of the first temple, some such offerings must have formed a feature.

A number of commentators (Delcor, Wolff) and some English versions (NEB/REB) have followed LXX and repointed *'ābᵉlu* as *'bᵉlu*, giving an imperative, 'Mourn, you priests' instead of the indicative of MT, 'The priests mourn'. Such a change fits well the general context of a summons to lament, but it is not always obvious that ancient authors were as concerned with formal correctness as some modern scholars. In any case, the view of the priests here is markedly different from that found in Hosea, where they are severely condemned (4.4; 6.9 and elsewhere). However close may be the links between successive books in the Minor Prophets, there are also important differences between them.

1.10. The powerful word-play in the Hebrew of this verse is liable to defeat any English rendering. So NRSV 'the fields are devastated' represents *šuddad śādeh*, 'the ground mourns' renders *'abᵉlāh ᵃdāmāh*, and 'the wine dries up' is for *hobiš tiroš*. In vv. 10-12 there are four different uses of the verbs *bōš* and *yābeš*. They are separate verbs meaning 'be dismayed' and 'dry up', but they are very close in sound, and there seems little doubt that the poet took great delight in using his skill to convey the horrors of the devastation. **Grain, wine** and **oil** form a standard triad to describe prosperity, and here again it seems likely that there may be a conscious reworking of older traditions. Deuteronomy

7.13, where these fruits are to be the reward of obedience to God in the promised land, may be in mind, but intertextuality within the Book of the Twelve may suggest that Hosea 2.8 (MT 2.10) provides the link here. For these blessings to be cut off, as is here pictured, is not only a deprivation in itself; it is a powerful symbol of the withdrawal of the Lord's favour. At 2.19, elaborated at 2.24, we shall have a picture of that favour renewed.

1.11. The summons to lament continues and is extended to those directly responsible for the crops. To describe *'ikkārim* as **farmers** may give slightly too exalted an impression of their social standing; the parallel with **vinedressers** (cf. Isa. 61.5) shows that those addressed were responsible for mundane agricultural tasks. Their exact status is a minor matter; more basic is the prophetic assertion that the disasters cause them to **wail** (the same verb, */h-l-l,* as in v. 5, though here spelt slightly differently in its plene form).

1.12. This verse is in effect a recapitulation and repetition of v. 7; as we saw there, the **vine** and the **fig tree** symbolized the prosperity of the community. Now, no doubt for rhetorical effect, three more fruits are mentioned: **pomegranate,** (date-)**palm** and *tappuaḥ,* the exact identity of which is disputed. The root *n-p-ḥ* seems to imply something scented; the conventional translation as **apple** seems unlikely, since the apple was not known in Israel in biblical times. 'Apricot' or 'quince' have been proposed as more likely identifications.

The first three trees are found also, in the same order, at Hagg. 2.19, and this has led Nogalski (1993a: 276-77) to cite it in evidence of his thesis that Joel is best understood through the part it played in building up the structure of the Book of the Twelve. One of the difficulties with this proposal, as Nogalski himself shows elsewhere (1993b: 177) is that this juxtaposition of the different trees is common to many parts of the Hebrew Bible. The verse reads like a kind of reversal of harvest thanksgiving; all the features of 'the land flowing with milk and honey' set out in a passage like Deut. 8.7-10, are here overthrown. The joy promised there is now to **wither away**.

It is striking that throughout the passage thus far no indication has been given as to the real cause of these disasters. Not before v. 15, with the introduction of the 'day of the Lord' theme, will divine causality begin to be spelt out.

1.13. The lament reaches a climax, with the more general summons now becoming specific; it is addressed in particular to the **priests** and

ministers of the altar. Unusually the summons to wear **sackcloth** is expressed by the verb alone; they are to **put on**, but what is to be put on is left to the imagination. It would be unwise to stress the apparent inconsistency between the rites required in v. 9 and those commanded here (thus Ahlstrom 1971); the passage should be seen as a whole, with the tension built up for dramatic effect. But the passage looks forward as well as back; the **grain offering and drink offering**, here **withheld**, will be available at 2.14. That verse, set in the context of confidence in God's ultimate forgiveness, forms an *inclusio* with the present passage, which stresses immediate evils.

1.14. The call to lament reaches its conclusion with a summons to fast. Fasting has played a part in the observances of many religious communities, but in Israel it seems to have been a matter of particular concern in the Second Temple period. Isaiah 58 warns of the dangers of wrongly motivated fasts; Zech. 7.1-7; 8.18-19 describes disputes in the early years of the Second Temple community about the proper time for fasting; and this passage fits into the same pattern, though it lacks any of the questioning note that is characteristic of the other texts. Here it is taken for granted that to **sanctify a fast** is the only possible response that the community can offer in the face of the disasters that have come upon it. The idea of a **solemn assembly** (*'āṣārāh*) is not new, but whereas in Amos 5.21 the solemn assemblies offered no delight to God, and in Isaiah 1.13 they were associated with iniquity, here it is assumed that such a gathering can hope to win divine favour. The reference to **elders** and **inhabitants of the land** provides a link back to v. 2. One of the most characteristic features of Joel is this pattern of intricate cross-reference. It should warn us against too precise a classification of the material, distinguishing sharply between sections addressed to limited groups and those concerned with all the people.

1.15. With this verse a new theme is introduced which is to be one of those most characteristic of the book of Joel: the **day of the Lord**. The shift in person, from a summons *to* the assembly to a cry apparently uttered *by* the assembly, suggests that we now have before us part of the laments that have been required. The somewhat jerky style of the next few verses may indicate that only fragments of the laments have been preserved (thus Wolff), or may be a deliberate literary device to express the incoherence of the lamenters in the face of the trouble that has come upon them.

The obvious starting point when considering 'day of the Lord'

language is Amos 5.18. There it would appear that the expectation of
the community had been that the day would be one of great blessing to
them, an expectation which the book of Amos is at pains to put right.
Here the community is not pictured as lulled by any false illusions of
that nature; the day of the Lord is associated with **destruction**. This
brings to mind a link of a rather different kind. The expression here
found, **the day of the Lord is near**, occurs in identical form (*qārōb
yōm yhwh*) several times in the Prophets. Some of those occurrences are
within the Book of the Twelve (Obad. 15; Zeph. 1.7, 14), but it is also
found at Isa. 13.6 and Ezek. 30.2, which will warn us against limiting
the literary context of Joel to the Book of the Twelve. The linkage with
Isa. 13.6 is particularly close. Indeed the whole sentence,

> For the day of the Lord is near,
> and as destruction from the Almighty it comes

is found in identical form in the Hebrew of that verse (NRSV has
slightly altered the word order). It is generally assumed that the Isaiah
passage is earlier. Its reference to Babylon makes it unlikely to go back
to any eighth-century original, but it is usually thought to be earlier than
Joel. If that is so, the quotation on Joel's part has undergone an interesting development. Whereas it had previously expressed a hope of
Yahweh's destruction being wreaked on a foreign enemy, here it is
acknowledged that it is liable to come upon his own followers.

The situation is somewhat further complicated by the close links
between this passage and Ezek. 30.2, which also has the phrase **Alas
for the day** (the same word for 'alas' is used, though spelt differently),
and warns of the nearness of that day. We have here a good example of
the problem touched upon in the Introduction. It is possible to see in
this usage a deliberate quotation from earlier texts as a literary device.
It is also possible, and perhaps on this occasion more likely, in view of
the frequency of the usage, that we have here a cultic fragment,
reflected in different prophetic collections. It may well have been a
form of words used in the temple cult, and the seriousness of such
utterances is now being underlined. Because it seems clear that Joel is
making use of a long-established tradition, whether literary or cultic, it
is probably unnecessary here to go in detail into the vexed question of
the origin of the 'Day of the Lord' tradition. Many proposals have been
made, such as links with holy war or with some form of cultic celebra-
tion, but no agreement has been reached, and unless some fresh evidence is unearthed it seems unlikely that it will be.

1.16. There are no specific references to the destruction wrought by locusts in this section, but the image of **food** being **cut off** certainly evokes the devastation they had caused. **Joy and gladness** should be characteristic of worship in the temple, but they too have been swept away. Since there are still those who retain the once-common imagery of Second Temple Judaism as characterized solely by anxious striving to keep the Law, the reference to 'joy and gladness' can serve as an important reminder of a very different reality.

1.17. The sense of this and of the next verse is clear in general terms. Together they picture the devastation of the regular pattern of agricultural life. The detail is, however, very far from clear, because several of the terms used are of uncertain meaning. As long ago as 1912 Bewer regarded the present form of the text as hopelessly corrupt, and supposed that the second half of the verse was simply a repetition of the first half, as far as the ancient scribe was able to make sense of it (Bewer 1912: 88-91). Allen (1976: 61) spoke of 'an amazing variety of suggestions' which have been put forward to clarify this section. They can only be speculative; 'an honest exegete will have to acknowledge that he is faced with an insoluble problem' (Prinsloo 1985: 29, gender-specificity in original).

The first word *'abašu* is the verb, but it occurs only here and its meaning is not certain. The meaning 'shrivel' has been that most commonly proposed, but it is noteworthy that the Qumran scroll (4QXIIc) has *'apašu*, which is also of uncertain meaning. This would suggest either an uncertainty on the part of early scribes, or that the text which has come down to us is corrupt. In any case, what has shrivelled? The *pᵉrudōt*, whatever they may be! They are usually taken to be grains of **seed**, but this meaning is only arrived at from the requirements of the context. The word is found in only one other place in the Hebrew Bible: Ezek. 1.11, where the context seems to require something like the NRSV translation 'wings'. A root *p-r-d*, meaning 'to divide' is well-known; BDB 825b uses this with hesitation to attain 'grains', since they are 'separated'; KBL 776b rejects any connection with that root and offers the meaning 'dried figs' (!). The uncertainty is an ancient one, as Wolff's survey (1977: 19) of the versional evidence shows.

Difficulties extend into the next phrase. The word **under** seems clear enough, though as we shall see in a moment, emendations have been proposed. But there follows another hapax legomenon: *megrᵉpōtehem*. A verb *garap* is found in the Song of Deborah (Judg. 5.21) meaning 'sweep away', and both BDB 175b and DCH (*sub* g-r-p) offer the meaning 'shovel' for our word, as the instrument for sweeping away. But BDB notes the traditional Jewish understanding 'clods' and recognizes that 'the meaning of the clause is dubious'. An additional problem arises from the fact that *megr^{e}pōtehem* looks very similar to the word *mamrugot*, **grain**, in the following line. Textual critics have suspected 'vertical dittography', that is, that one of these forms has infected the other and that one of them has been written erroneously. Literary critics tend rather to favour the view that such similarities are deliberate and reflect the author's poetic skill.

As has just been noted the one word in this clause that seems clear in its meaning is *tahat*, 'under'. But BHS has suggested that the context requires a verb, and proposes an emendation to *hattu*. A similar emendation is noted as a possibility by DCH, which suggests a verb *hatat* meaning 'be dry' and found in Jer. 14.4 and here. This was the reasoning which underlay the NEB emendation of MT *tahat* to *tehat*, giving the translation 'the dykes are dry'. (For reasons unknown to me, whereas NEB usually offers detailed footnotes setting out its variations from the Hebrew text, Joel 1.1–2.22 are completely free of such notes.)

In this situation certainty is impossible. Fortunately the broad sense of the clause is clear, and it seems best to agree with Barthélemy (1992), who concludes an extended note (pp. 628-32) by describing this as 'a very difficult passage in which no other textual form seems preferable to MT'.

The remainder of the verse seems more straightforward. It is clearly a picture of the complete disruption of the usual agricultural pattern, with **storehouses** and **granaries** not only lacking their usual contents, but reduced to ruin. The word translated 'granaries' provides one of the relatively rare examples in the Hebrew Bible where different manuscripts offer different spellings. The base manuscript of BHS, given the siglum 'L' for 'Leningrad' when it was published (its designation has since undergone various changes), has *mamm^{e}gurōt*. Other manuscripts omit the initial 'm' and it is likely that an error, dittography, has crept into L at this point.

1.18. The picture of agricultural desolation is concluded by describing the misery to which the animals are subjected. It would be very misleading to detect any 'animal rights' thinking in the Hebrew Bible, but the livestock are very much assumed to be part of the whole of creation which is suffering under the devastation the community is undergoing. Only here do animals **groan**; it is the same verb, *'ānaḥ*, as is used of the groaning of the Israelites under Egyptian bondage (Exod. 2.23). The last word, noted in NRSV margin as 'Meaning of Heb. uncertain', may be an only occurrence of the niphal (passive) form of the common verb *'ašam*, 'be guilty'. In this case one understanding would be that the sheep are 'suffering because of Israel's guilt' (DCH I 415a), an interesting picture of corporate responsibility. But many have supposed that another verb, probably *šāmam*, should be understood here, and a translation 'waste away' or the like, be adopted.

1.19. A double shift here takes place. First, the form is a prayer of lament; secondly, it is expressed in the first person singular, the first time that this is used in the book. The shift to singular form has the effect of intensifying the lament which has already been in progress since v.15. In both form and language this first-person singular material is very reminiscent of the individual laments in the Psalms, where it also may be interspersed with plural passages, as in e.g. Psalm 130. The theme of calling (*qārā'*) upon God in time of trouble is found several times in the Psalms (e.g. 50.15; 81.7 [MT 81.8]). The cause of the lament differs both from what is found in any surviving Psalms and from what has been mentioned previously in this chapter. We need not ask how fire could consume pastures. More important is the vivid poetic effect, increased by alliteration (*lehābāh liḥ^atāh*), in the account of how the **flames have burned**.

1.20. At first sight this verse reads awkwardly in the Hebrew for the plural subject (**wild animals**) is followed by a singular verb (**cry**). Actually, however, this kind of usage is not unknown in Hebrew, and the BHS proposal to emend either to a singular subject or to a plural verb is a tentative one, with a note that similar usage is also found in 2.22. More doubtful is the verb itself: the verb *'ārāg* is found at Ps. 42.1 (MT 42.2), its only other occurrence, with the sense of 'long for' and an animal subject, and that sense is retained in REB ('look to you'). Most versions (as far back as the AV, itself dependent on rabbinic tradition) have preferred the sense 'cry', which offers a good parallel with the preceding verse. It is striking that the same verse of the Psalm also contains the reference to **watercourses** found here: another example of the 'briefer parallels and allusions' to other biblical passages mentioned in the Introduction. The verse ends by repeating in almost identical form the expression in 19a.

2.1. The poetic quality of 2.1-11 was chosen by Alter (1990: 40-43) as a parade example of the characteristics of Hebrew poetry. He stresses the way in which the poet imparts 'the rhythm of an inexorable march to his description of the advancing enemy army'.

The opening phrase provides an obvious link with Hos. 5.8. There a repeated expression served as a summons 'to blow the horn in Gibeah, the trumpet in Ramah'; here the trumpet (*šōpār*) is to be sounded in Zion itself. The *šōpār* might be used as a summons to festal occasions; here its function clearly is as a warning to those who hear it, as is brought out by the second verb, *hārî'u*, **sound the alarm**. Once again there is a link with Hos. 5.8. It is surely right here to see a deliberate literary link, stressing the fact that the threat once associated with other sanctuaries is now directed against **Zion**, God's own **holy mountain**. This is the first specific reference in the book to Zion, but it will pervade the remainder of Joel. Both in MT and in the NRSV translation the book closes with the word 'Zion'.

This brings back and as it were localizes the theme already expressed in 1.15—**the day of the Lord**. What was there hinted at is now spelt out in greater detail, linking the theme of enemy attack with allusions to that day. (The inter-relationship is worked out in detail by Bergler 1988: 49-52, though he makes nothing of the link with Hos. 5.8.)

2.2. Whether or not the last phrase of v. 1 (**it is near**) is formally combined with v. 2 (so BHS), it clearly belongs there in sense, and is a further link with 1.15. It also provides another link with other prophetic texts, for Zeph. 1.14-15 also emphasizes that 'the great day of the Lord is near'. Indeed that whole section of Zephaniah can be seen as closely related to Joel 2.1-2. As in many other passages we are faced with the possibility of either a cultic or a literary linkage, or, of course, both. In addition we are faced with the choice of stressing the similarities between Joel and Zephaniah, and thus placing Joel within an on-going prophetic tradition, or emphasizing the differences, in which case Joel may more appropriately be seen as 'proto-apocalyptic' (Cook 1995: 171-75).

The four descriptions of the day which now follow are virtually synonymous; they are piled on top of each other for greater effect. The links with the stress on **darkness** in Amos's warnings about the day (5.18) are unmistakable. What follows in the Hebrew text is unexpected. It is represented by RV 'as the dawn spread upon the mountains'. But dawn is regularly in the Hebrew Bible a sign of new hope after the dispersion of the darkness, and there are no other signs of hope in this passage. BHS and most modern translations, including NRSV, have therefore emended *š^{a}ḥar* ('dawn') to *š^{e}ḥōr* ('**blackness**', or, as in Lam. 4.8, 'soot'). This may be right, but it is unusual to speak of **blackness spread upon the mountains**; that is the usual way of speaking of dawn. Since both the Hebrew and the ancient versional evidence are unanimously in favour of 'dawn' as the correct reading, perhaps the sense here is that even the dawn, normally a time of renewed hope, will prove to be a 'false dawn', for it will reveal the **great and powerful army**, somewhat in the manner described in narrative form in Judg. 9.34-41. (Barthélemy 1992: 632-33 recommends a reading in this sense; Alter 1990 has 'like soot' in his translation, but leaves both possibilities open in his comments.)

It would be a misdirection of energy to enquire whether the **army** is intended as a precise reference to the locusts of ch. 1. That picture will clearly be in the reader's or hearer's mind, and thereby will add to the overwhelming impression of terror brought about by the description. The last two lines of the verse are a standard way of expressing the magnitude of a disaster in the Hebrew Bible. For example, the hail which was one of the plagues of Egypt was such 'as had never fallen in all the land of Egypt' (Exod. 9.24).

2.3. The picture of **fire** and **flame** recalls 1.19, where very similar phraseology is used. Much more unexpected is the reference to **the garden of Eden**. Here very clearly an allusion is being made to a topos which would already be familiar to the reader or hearer. Less certain is whether the reference is to Genesis 2, as would seem natural to the biblically-educated modern reader. More likely is a reference to Ezekiel's use of this theme. In the 'lamentation over the king of Tyre' (Ezek. 28.11-19) we find a contrast similar to that outlined here, from the former exalted state 'in Eden, the garden of God' (v. 13) to 'a dreadful end' (v. 19). Again in Ezek. 36.35 the contrast theme is expressed, but in reverse order from that found in Joel. In Ezekiel that which was formerly 'desolate has become like the garden of Eden'. This reversal of an established picture is also applicable when we compare our verse with Isa. 51.3, where the wilderness was to become 'like Eden, her desert like the garden of the Lord'. Here, as in 3.10 (MT 4.10), we have the reversal of a passage from Isaiah—another warning that we should not limit our picture of the literary development of Joel to the Book of the Twelve.

The last clause, **and nothing escapes them**, well illustrates different

approaches to the understanding of the Hebrew Bible. For BHS it is a
metrically awkward addition; for Alter the whole verse is a 'brilliant
exploitation' of the possibilities of surprise inherent in the parallelism.

2.4. There is little point in asking whether the reference is still to
locusts. The range of figurative language is extended by the introduction of a new comparison which will dominate the next short section;
that with **horses** and chariots. The language is built up, from the ordinary horses of the first phrase to the **war-horses** of the second. Not sur-
prisingly, when horses are the subject of comparison, the nature of the
verbs now changes, so that what is seen is not only the horses themselves but the fact that they **charge**.

2.5. The vigorous momentum introduced at the end of the previous
verse is dominant here. The horses are accompanied by **chariots**, which
are said to skip (*yᵉraqqedun*) **on the tops of the mountains**. The second half of the verse offers a different, but equally destructive, simile:
that of **fire**. The picture of the attackers comes to a climax with the
likeness to a **powerful army drawn up for battle**.

2.6. Attention shifts briefly from the threat itself to those who are
threatened. These are not some small group; the threat extends to **peoples**, which may in effect stand for everyone. They **are in anguish**, the
verb (*ḥil*) being that commonly used for women in childbirth. The
meaning of the second clause is uncertain (see NRSV margin); as long
ago as 1907 BDB 803a listed a variety of proposals and regarded them
as 'all very uncertain'. But it would be unwise to suggest any emendation, for the same phrase is found at Nah. 2.10 (MT 2.11). The question
obviously arises whether we should here, as so often in Joel, detect
dependence on another text. Bergler (1988: 139) pointed out similarities
between both these texts and Isa. 13.6-7, but notes that our particular
phrase is peculiar to Nahum and Joel.

2.7. We return to the threat. Now it is likened to an army, inexorable
in its attack. To those within the army itself, much may seem to be
muddle and confusion, but to those who are threatened by it all is rigor-
ously organized: the charge, the capacity to overcome obstacles in the
path. The difficult word in this verse is *yᵉʿabbᵉtūn*, rendered 'do not
swerve from' in NRSV. The footnote there notes that the normal sense
of the Hebrew would be 'do not take a pledge along', and BHS accepts
the text without any marginal note. Barthélemy (1992: 633-35) is very
emphatic ('Note "A"') that the Masoretic Text is to be accepted. He
claims that the sense that the components of the army do not exchange

places can be obtained from the Hebrew, citing several mediaeval
Jewish commentators. At times this is more ingenious than convincing,
but the various other versions cited by NRSV seem themselves to have
been uncertain of the meaning. Clearly some demonstration of army
discipline is envisaged here.

2.8. To the helpless defenders the oncoming army appears to be perfectly organized. They don't get in one another's way. In the second
half of the verse we have another picture of the uselessness of any
defensive measure. NRSV translates *šelaḥ* as 'weapons', and this may be
right. But several commentators (Rudolph, Allen) have detected here an
allusion to 'Shiloah', the stream whose rivers 'flow gently' in Isa. 8.5.
If that is so, then the underlying idea might be that the aqueduct of
Shiloh was, like everything else tried, useless as a deterrent. The last
phrase also poses problems as to its precise meaning, though the general sense of an unstoppable onrush is clear enough. BHS holds that the
Hebrew *lo' yibṣa'u* may be corrupt, and proposes an emendation to a
form of the verb *b-q-'*, 'break open', linking it with 'the city', which is
the first word in the Hebrew text of v. 9. But this seems to be a purely
speculative emendation, and it is better to stay with the text. The normal
meaning of *b-ṣ-'*, 'cut off' yields tolerable sense: 'they do not cut off
(their course)', that is, they are unstoppable.

2.9. In the course of this verse the figurative language becomes more
appropriate for locusts than for a human army. Thus the verb *šāqaq*,
here translated 'leap', is specifically applied to locusts at Isa. 33.4,
although we should note that at Nah. 2.4 (MT 2.5) it is used of chariots
which 'rush to and fro'. The proposal that the reference to **the walls**
implies that their rebuilding under Nehemiah, c. 433 BCE, had already
taken place, seems very dubious. We have already noted several times
how dangerous it is to claim to read off historical allusions from the
kind of poetry we find in Joel.

At the end of the verse we have the picture of a **thief** entering a home
through the window. This metaphor is most commonly used in the
Bible to denote secret wrongdoing, but there is nothing secret about this
invasion. Crenshaw (1995: 125) suggests that there may be an allusion
here to the final visitant—death—whose entry 'through the window'
was a familiar topos in ancient mythology (cf. Jer. 9.21 [MT 9.20]).

2.10. An indication is offered that the poem is nearing its conclusion
by the reference back to the beginning. The verb *rāgaz*, here 'quakes',
was used in v. 1 (there translated 'tremble'). It is not simply the inhab-

itants of the earth who tremble; the very earth itself quakes. We are being made to realize that what is being envisaged extends beyond locusts and a human army to the whole created order: **earth**, **heavens**, **sun**, **moon** and **stars**. The whole normal pattern of events is transformed. This is the language of the apocalypses, and indeed it used to be common among commentators to see vv. 10-11 as a later addition by a later editor from the 'apocalyptic period'. But the whole section, 2.1-11, is best seen as a unity that builds up to a powerful climax.

2.11. Whether pictured as locusts, the advance of an army or the break-up of the created order, this final verse of the poem makes it clear that what is envisaged is the work of Yahweh himself. He is in control of all that is pictured. The point is brought out in the Hebrew by the divine name being placed at the beginning of the verse for emphasis. This verse, like the earlier part of the poem, has links with Isaiah 13, where the basic theme is similar; this is one of the many places in Joel where it appears as if part of the poet's intention was to make applicable to his own day the oracles of an earlier and revered collection. (Curiously Nogalski, despite his detailed examination of the literary indebtedness of Joel, makes no reference to Isa. 13.) In both passages the 'Day of the Lord' is pictured in terms of the gathering of a mighty host to carry out judgment of cosmic proportions.

Thus this poem is completed. All are agreed on the power of its poetic imagery, and it is likely too that we should see here a skilful re-application of earlier material to make it relevant to what the author of Joel regarded as important for his own day. No doubt the application of what in Isaiah 13 had been directed against foreign enemies to the people of Yahweh themselves also teaches a powerful lesson.

When all this is said and done, however, a feeling of uneasiness must surely remain for the modern reader. It is striking that none of the commentaries that have been consulted appear to display any disquiet about the understanding of God here displayed. Locusts and armies are powerful symbols of destruction, and the author is not afraid to portray God as willing to break up the very creation he has ordered. At the very least contemporary readers, particularly if they are religous believers, ought surely to be asking whether language of this kind tells them more about the nature of God or about the negative impulses of the poet.

2.12-14. Though the overarching theme of lament in the face of impending disaster remains, this section differs formally from what has preceded. It is a summons to repentance, using the language of weeping that was found already in 1.13. It is interesting that in much modern Christian worship practice such language is once again coming to be taken literally. We need not doubt that **weeping** and **mourning**, as envisaged here, played an integral part in the worship of ancient Israel.

The passage as a whole is in fact a curious mixture. Sometimes as in v. 12 the various ritual gestures are to be understood literally; in v. 13, by contrast, the rending of clothes is less important than the commitment of the mind which is envisaged in **rend your hearts**. (The precise practicalities of 'rending' one's garments have never been satisfactorily explained; presumably some kind of ritual tear in the fringe of the garment, rather than its literal destruction, should be envisaged.) The whole phrase ('Rend your hearts and not your garments' in the language of the older translations) has come to be seen by many, especially in some Protestant traditions, as a kind of epitome of prophetic teaching, the suggestion being that rending of garments may be nothing more than a mere outward gesture.

In fact if one were to look for an epitome of a good deal of Hebrew Bible thought about Yahweh it can better be found in the second half of the verse. This quasi-credal affirmation is found, in slightly variant form, in numerous passages: Exod. 34.6; Num. 14.18; Jon. 4.2; Nah. 1.3; several passages in the Psalms (e.g. 86.15); 2 Chron. 30.9; and Neh. 9.17—these by no means exhaust all the allusions, but give an indication of how widely this understanding of Yahweh and his character is found. It is impossible to decide, in the face of such widespread usage, whether our verse is better understood as reflecting liturgical practice or as an allusion to one or more of the other passages mentioned. Bolin (1997: 169-72) has noted that there are especially close links between Joel and Jon. 4.2, drawing attention particularly to the fact that these texts invert the more common order ('merciful and gracious') and each have **gracious and merciful**, and add the phrase **and relents from punishing**. He goes on to argue, against what he claims to be the more commonly held view of Joel's priority, that Joel was dependent on Jonah.

Fishbane had already suggested that one reason for the constant re-iteration of this language about God was the need to emphasize the belief that Yahweh was gracious and merciful, as well as an enforcer of justice. Humans might never be able to discern the reasons for such mercy, but it was an integral element of their belief (Fishbane 1985: 335-50, esp. 346-47).

A feature of descriptions of this kind is the possibility raised in both Joel and Jonah that God may actually change his mind: he may **relent from punishing**. For the picture of God that has been normative in the Christian tradition such a thought would raise acute philosophical problems, but it seems not to have been perceived as a difficulty by religious writers in ancient Israel. In this, as in many other respects, they were quite content with an anthropomorphic presentation of God. Just as a great ruler might condescend to forgive erring subjects who deserved punishment, so, it was averred, might God overlook the strict requirements of justice. It could only be a hope, expressed here with a wistful **Who knows?** This provides another link with Jonah, for it is the same expression as that put into the mouth of the king of Nineveh (Jon. 3.9), where also the possibility that God might **turn and relent** (*yāšub wᵉnihām*—the same expression as is found here) is set out.

The section ends with a curious picture. The **grain offering and drink offering**, already mentioned in 1.9 as no longer featuring as part of the people's worship, are here presented as if they are at least part of the **blessing** which God leaves **behind him**. BHS suggests that the text may have been corrupted by the omission of a verb which would make it clear that these were the people's offerings. Perhaps in poetry a measure of ellipsis of the kind found here is acceptable.

2.15-16. Verses 12-14 are best seen as a kind of interjection setting out the possibilities which it was legitimate for the community to hope for. Now we return to the series of imperatives. Verse 15 uses expressions already found in 2.1 and 1.14, but now the imperatives are extended. The emphasis is on the need for the whole religious community to be brought together before its God. '*am*, **people,** is one of the commonest of Hebrew words, but here it is more limited in meaning than elsewhere; it is in synonymous parallelism with *qāhāl*, used more specifically of a religious **congregation**. The only special significance which we should note in the groups singled out is their all-encompassing nature: not only the **aged** but even the youngest of **children** are to be summoned, as are those whose minds might be thought to be on other things: **bridegroom** and **bride**.

2.17. When everyone is assembled the **priests'** responsibilities are now spelt out. The setting is clearly that of the Jerusalem temple: its constituent parts are differently described in different translations (REB here has 'porch and altar'), but the overall picture is clear. We are used to thinking of the temple as a place of sacrifice; here we are reminded that it was also a place of prayer (cf. Isa. 56.7). The first requirement of the priests is that they should **weep**. Tears in religious worship were until quite recent times regarded in much of the modern Western tradition as something of an embarrassment, but they are taken for granted in the biblical tradition—so much so, that it is difficult to know when a particular reference is a metaphor or is describing actual weeping. There are numerous references to weeping in Jeremiah (e.g. 3.21; 13.17), and it is clear that the Jeremiah tradition regarded weeping as a necessary and proper response to the evils that the community was experiencing. To speak of weeping as a display of emotion, as many modern discussions do, is to miss the point; professional weepers had an important part to play in ceremonies of lament. (See the extended discussion in Hvidberg 1962.)

The structure of the lament and the theme it raises are close to the lament Psalms (e.g. Ps. 44.9-16 [MT 10-17]). Not only is an appeal to be made for God to show mercy in their time of trouble; there is also more than a hint of blackmail in the terms of the prayer. If God does not act, not only will his **heritage** become a **mockery**, but observers will put his inaction down to inadequacy: **'Where is their God'** is clearly envisaged as a mocking question. The same question is found in another lament Psalm (Ps. 79.10), of which our verse is almost a quotation (the word **peoples** [*'ammim*] here replaces 'nations' [*goyim*], which the Psalmist had used in the previous strophe). The literary technique is well-known for its use in narrative form by Moses when God threatens to abandon the people in the wilderness in Numbers 14; cf. especially v. 16.

2.18-19. In more senses than one we have here a new start. Not only does this section provide an answer to the preceding lament, but it also switches from the direct address of the preceding verses to third-person narrative account, as if the writer were distant from the events he is describing. Traces of this device can be found in subsequent verses (e.g. v. 23), but most of what follows is presented as direct first-person speech by God himself, so that it is difficult to descry a consistent pattern. In addition, though this section is printed as poetry in both BHS and NRSV, it is by no means certain that it should be regarded as poetry. It is not easy to discern an underlying metric pattern, and several forms usually associated with prose are present, for example the use of the direct object marker *-eth*, often regarded as confined to prose usage, is found before 'grain' (v. 19) and 'the northern army' (v. 20). B. Duhm is said to have regarded the rest of the book as a prose elaboration of the basic text, but such a view would rarely be found in recent writing (Prinsloo 1985: 63).

God's action is set out in such a way as clearly to imply that the prayer itself has 'worked', in the sense of convincing God that something had to be done about the situation; what he does is **in response to his people**. The word **jealous** has such negative connotations in modern English that it scarcely seems appropriate here, where God's response is presented positively: REB 'showed his ardent love' is a very free translation, but brings out the sense well.

As in other prophetic collections (cf. for example Zech. 8.12-13), we are here confronted with a reversal of earlier threats of disaster. The reference to **grain, wine and oil** offers an obvious link back to 1.10, where these staples of life had been exhausted; now they will be provided to the point of satiety (**you will be satisfied** is something of an under-translation). God says nothing about the possibility of **the nations** mocking *him*, but the threat against his people is to be removed. The *ḥerpāh*, **mockery**, is found both in the mouth of individuals (e.g. the Philistine giant in 1 Sam. 17.26 [NRSV 'reproach']) and of nations (e.g. Ezek. 36.15 [NRSV 'disgrace of the peoples']).

2.20. The word *haṣṣᵉpōni* has been much discussed; Kapelrud devoted a 15-page excursus to this verse, discussing both text- and literary-critical issues (1948: 93-108). He concluded that the text could be retained, so that NRSV rendering **the northern army** is acceptable. Some commentators (e.g. Allen) have seen here another reference to locusts, and it may not be a fatal objection to that view to point out that locusts did not come from that direction. Nevertheless, because of the many links we have already found between Joel and other parts of the Hebrew Bible, it seems more likely that we have here an allusion to the material in Jeremiah (e.g. 6.22-23) and elsewhere, threatening destruction by invaders from the North. Kapelrud wished to combine this sense with a 'mythical element'. In any case, we must not expect to find exact geography in this material: **the eastern sea** could be the Dead Sea, but it seems more natural to see here a picture of the total destruction of those who set themselves up as God's enemies. Whether it be into **a parched and desolate land** or into the sea, envisaged here as so often in the Hebrew Bible as an alien element, the inevitability and totality of their destruction is set out.

The next part of the verse may well be a prose elaboration, but it is in any case not easy to make a clear distinction between poetry and prose throughout this section. We need to remember that the distinction between prose and poetry in classical Hebrew is not always a sharp one.

The word translated **foul smell**, *ṣaḥanāto*, occurs only here in the Hebrew Bible, so that older translators had to work out its sense from the context. It has however now been found in the Hebrew text of Sirach (11.12), and in any case the parallel with *bā'oš*, **stench**, leaves little room for doubt.

NRSV takes the last line of the verse to be a reference to the **great things** wrought by Yahweh, and this sense would be even clearer if we followed the proposal of BHS that the divine name should be inserted, as it is in the similar phrase in v. 21. Wolff supposed that the similarity with v. 21 was best explained by seeing here an erroneous doublet from that verse, offering the curious translation 'for he has acted great'. Allen took it to be a reference to the defeated enemy, translating 'because of their high and mighty deeds', but it is unlikely that the same phrase would be used in successive verses to refer first to the enemies and then to Yahweh. It is probably best to stick with MT; a link is thereby offered to the next oracle.

2.21-24. We move to an oracle of salvation. All are to join in the praise of God, beginning here with the **soil**, leading on to **the animals of the field** and reaching a climax with the **children of Zion** in v. 23. The command '**Do not fear**' is of course most commonly addressed to a human audience, especially kings, as Conrad 1985 has shown. Here, however, all the orders of creation are to join together in acknowledging God's saving acts.

Much of what follows is most readily understood as a reversal of the conditions of devastation pictured earlier, and there are frequent cross-references with earlier parts of the book. Thus in 1.19 the **pastures of the wilderness** were devoured by fire; here they are not merely restored, but transformed so that now they positively 'sprout' (*daš'ū*): NRSV '**are green**'. Similarly the **fig tree and vine**, devastated at 1.12, are now restored to their full strength. 'Strength' is the natural meaning of *ḥēlām* (so AV here; NRSV, **their full yield**, conveys the sense, though perhaps less poetically. More generally, the withering away of joy at 1.12 is now dramatically brought to an end, so that the people are twice invited (vv. 21, 23) to **be glad and rejoice**.

With **children of Zion** at the beginning of v. 23 the concern of NRSV for inclusive language obscures an unusual feature in the Hebrew. The

expression 'Daughter Zion' is frequently found as referent or addressee
in the Hebrew Bible, and it is the identification of Zion with the daughter that is the usual sense, so that the traditional translation 'Daughter(s)
of Zion' is somewhat misleading. Here, however, the Hebrew has 'sons
of Zion' (thus RSV); it does not seem as if any special significance
underlies the change of usage; REB 'people of Zion' gets the sense.

The metaphor then changes. Whereas it has previously been concerned either with enemy invasion or with the attacks of locusts, now it
switches to drought. The fall of rain will bring relief. The **early rain**
(*mōreh*) is similarly described at Ps. 84.6 (MT 84.7), though oddly the
reading is suspect in each case. The form is usually *yōreh*, and in our
present verse the description seems curiously overloaded. BHS proposes drastic surgery, reducing the divine gift to 'he has given you
rain'; NEB/REB have also emended the verse, omitting the reference to
early and later rain, with the curious phrase in the NEB footnote 'Heb.
adds', as if what was being discussed was something other than the
Hebrew text. On the other hand it is not difficult to see the elaboration
as a way of summoning thanksgiving for the essential gift of rain, and
Barthélemy favours retaining MT.

An interesting feature is the reference to **vindication** (*ṣᵉdāqāh*). The
range of meaning of the *ṣ-d-q* root is considerable. It can refer to what
is right or appropriate, and this sense is taken up by REB to provide the
translation 'in due measure'. Another possibility is that favoured by
Allen, who notes that the root is often found in contexts that can
broadly be described as covenantal, and so he detects here the restoration of covenant harmony. The NRSV has the advantage of using the
word in the same general sense as is frequently found in the later chapters of Isaiah. In the Qumran Dead Sea Scrolls their leader is referred to
as *moreh ṣᵉdāqāh*, usually translated 'teacher of righteousness'. It has
been maintained that the Qumran covenanters deliberately used this
passage from Joel as descriptive of their leader (Roth 1963: 94-95), but
no surviving Qumran text refers to our passage. It is certainly possible
that this is one of the texts lying behind the Qumran usage, but this
must be regarded as an element in the history of interpretation rather
than anything that can help in direct exegesis.

For the last word of the verse a literal rendering would offer 'in the
beginning', but most translations have either made a conscious textual
modification, changing the inseparable Hebrew preposition, to produce
'as' for 'in', or have found that to be the only acceptable translation.

More difficult is to decide whether the sense is simply the restoration of normality, or whether **as before** implies something more profound, the true and basic order of creation. It may well be that we should see the account of creation in Genesis 1 as the background to this whole passage. The blessings envisaged amount to a new creation.

However that may be, more immediate practical concerns are not lacking. The section concludes by reiterating the promise of restoration, so that all the blessings of prosperous agricultural life will once again come to the people.

2.25. 'The years that the locust has eaten' has become something of a proverbial expression in English. The phrases used here to describe the various locusts are identical with those in 1.4. If this verse is taken as determinative for interpreting what has preceded, it establishes the fact that all the references to a **great army** have been to the ravages of the locusts. Whether such a rich variety of figurative language can be made to have so precise and limited a reference will continue to be disputed.

2.26-27. By comparison with the rich imagery which has characterized so much of Joel these two verses offer a rather conventional form of thanksgiving. The promise that the people will **eat in plenty** may seem deplorably materialistic to modern readers in the affluent West, but to a community ravaged by plagues and drought it was one of the surest signs of God's restored favour, and the Hebrew Bible is rich in promises of this kind, from the land 'flowing with milk and honey' of Exodus and Deuteronomy to the 'messianic banquet' of Isaiah 25. Some scholars have wished to delete one of the occurrences of '**And my people shall never again be put to shame**', seeing it as accidental repetition (thus BHS proposes deleting this clause at v. 26; this proposal was accepted by NEB, but the words have been restored in REB), but it is much more likely to be a deliberate repetition for emphasis. The section ends with the affirmation of a unique God and a uniquely blessed people. Both of the ways in which this is expressed **You shall know that I am in the midst of Israel** and **I, the Lord, am your God and there is no other** find close parallels in other prophetic collections (Ezek. 36.11 and Isa. 45.5-6, 18 were noted in the list in the introduction), and here it does seem that the use of a stock mode of expression is perhaps more likely than a deliberate allusion to a particular passage.

2.28 (MT 3.1). The short third chapter in the Hebrew text is regarded as the conclusion of ch. 2 in all English versions. It begins with what to Christian readers will perhaps be the best-known section of the whole book, for it was taken over by the author of the Acts of the Apostles. Peter, in his speech offering an explanation of the speaking with tongues which had been such a striking feature of the gathering at Pentecost, claimed that this was 'what was spoken through the prophet Joel' (Acts 2.16). It is somewhat unusual for any of the Minor Prophets to be mentioned specifically by name; for the most part in the New Testament period they were regarded as a unity, 'the Twelve'.

The notion of the pouring out of the divine **spirit** is another way in which Christian reading of this material has developed it. In the Christian tradition the time of Pentecost is associated with the giving of the Holy Spirit, which came to be identified as the third member in the Trinitarian picture of God. This meant that this verse has acquired major theological significance in Christian usage. In the context of the book of Joel itself, however, one should be cautious about making such claims; the 'spirit' or 'breath' (*ruaḥ*) of God was not prominent in what are conventionally described as 'the pre-exilic prophets', but from Ezekiel 37 onwards it played a major role in pictures of God's communication with human worshippers, and there are similarities between our passage and Ezek. 39.29.

In Ezekiel, however, the pouring out of the spirit is specifically confined to 'the house of Israel'. By contrast, one of the features in our text upon which Peter fastens in his address in Acts is that the promise are offered to **all flesh**. It suits the context of Acts very well; it is more surprising to find such a universalist notion in Joel itself, particularly with some of the language of ch. 3 (MT ch. 4) in mind. Here, however, the universality of the gift is stressed, and expressed in remarkable terms. First, the gift will be discerned through the fact that its recipients **shall prophesy**. In some quarters prophetism acquired a dubious reputation in the Second Temple period (e.g. Zech. 13.2-6), but not so here. This may provide incidental illustration of the way in which Joel was indebted to and made free use of other writings within the Prophets.

Secondly, the gift will be available to women: **daughters** are to prophesy. There are women prophets in the Hebrew Bible, occasionally favourably spoken of (e.g. Huldah, 2 Kgs 22.14), but mostly rejected by the male authors of the material (Ezek. 13.17; Neh. 6.14). Here their participation in the prophetic role seems to be greeted enthusiastically.

Thirdly, to **dream dreams** and to **see visions** is presented in positive terms. Again, this runs counter to other presentations. In Jeremiah 23, for example, the visions that the prophets speak are 'of their own minds' (v. 16) and a contrast is drawn between the dreamer and the one who has God's word (v. 26).

It is tempting but probably misguided to speculate on the sociological underpinning of passages like this. Many recent studies, following in particular the work of Hanson 1979, have explored the tensions within the religious community of Second Temple Judaism, and it is possible that the hopes expressed here are at some level a reaction to those tensions. But the vivid poetry in which they are expressed, together with the other uncertainties about the date and background of Joel, caution against such speculation. As with many other parts of Joel, it may be more useful to seek a literary rather than a sociological background for this passage, in which case Num. 11.29 is a likely source, with the claim being made that the wish expressed there was now about to be fulfilled.

2.29 (3.2). The various apocalyptic movements that developed in the last centuries BCE broke down many barriers, but we hear relatively little of the breaking down of social distinctions such as is envisaged here. We may suppose that the thought of **male and female slaves** being endued with the divine spirit is not something that would have been welcomed by the majority of their owners.

2.30-31 (3.3-4). Here we enter the visionary world commonly associated with the apocalypses. **Portents** of the kind described here are treated with suspicion in some of the New Testament writings (e.g. Mt. 12.39), but this kind of language is typical of the apocalyptic visions so important in one strand of Second Temple Judaism. But there may also be a backward look, for the word is also used of the mighty acts performed by Yahweh in delivering his people from Egypt. The word *mōpᵉtīm*, here 'portents', is the same as that rendered 'wonders' at Exod. 7.3, describing the devastation threatened against Egypt. (Bergler 1988: 268-73 discusses this and a number of other proposed links with the Exodus tradition.) Here it is expressed in the **day of the Lord** language that is prominent through much of Joel, though here the terror that was threatened against the people themselves in 2.1-11 is now transferred to enemies who will be identified more specifically in the remainder of the book. The day is described as **great and terrible**, the same manner of description as is found in Mal. 4.5 (MT 3.23). As with some of the earlier cross-references we have noted, it is doubtful whether this should be seen as a specific literary allusion.

In view of the uncertainty about the date of Joel it would be unwise to attempt to track down too precisely the manner in which this 'day of the Lord' imagery developed. We shall see when we come to Amos that it was envisaged by many as a time of rejoicing, a context which is supported by allusions to it in the Psalms (e.g. Ps. 118.24). This attitude is strongly condemned in Amos (5.18). But, whatever developments may have taken place liturgically, it increasingly became a literary trope in the later literature of the Hebrew Bible. In this passage it is striking that the various portents described, with **the sun...turned to darkness and the moon to blood**, take place **before** the day itself arrives. In other words the day of the Lord itself is raised to an even greater height, for which the most dreadful cosmic convulsions are no more than preliminary.

2.32 (3.5). But this presentation is itself no more than preliminary, for the message is after all a hopeful one, for **everyone who calls on the name of the LORD shall be saved**. This is a strand of thought that finds parallels in Zechariah (8.20-23; 14.16). Even at the risk of diminishing the vision, it is important to point out that this happy outcome is confined, both here and in the Zechariah passages, to those who worship at **Jerusalem**. Isaiah 4.2, almost certainly one of the later components of the early chapters of Isaiah, is another similar passage; it is those who 'are left in Zion and remain in Jerusalem' who receive the divine favour. We should probably not be wrong in seeing in this material a rejection of the claims of other sanctuaries. *yimmālet*, translated 'escape' in NRSV, also has the sense of being delivered.

As to the general sense of this verse there is little room for doubt, but its precise structure is less clear. Part of the difficulty is the preposition *bᵉ* before *śᵉrîdîm* (**survivors**). NRSV avoids the difficulty by translating the preposition as **among**. This may be right, though a better balance would be achieved by reordering the verse and moving the preposition so that we should have 'survivors in Jerusalem' to balance **those who escape in Mount Zion**. BHS, tentatively supported by some commentators (e.g. Allen), makes this proposal; as so often with rearrangements of this kind one is left wondering how the present, apparently less satisfactory, order arose. The position is here rendered more complex by the fact that the reference to those who escape is a direct quotation of, or at the very least an allusion to, Obadiah 17. This link with Obadiah is one of a series which we shall notice as we work through the final chapter of Joel.

3.1 (4.1). Whatever be thought of the differing Hebrew and English chapter arrangements earlier in the book, here we clearly have a new start, even though the first word in the Hebrew text (*ki*) most commonly refers back to what has preceded. Not infrequently, however, it is asseverative, making a strong assertion, and that seems to be the sense here. If we wanted to be literal we might translate 'Surely, behold, in those days'—three distinct calls to attention.

Nogalski (1993b: 26-57) provides a detailed analysis of Joel 4, which he divides into an introduction (vv. 1-3), an oracle against Tyre, Sidon and the Philistines (vv. 4-8), an eschatological call to judgment (vv. 9-17), and an eschatological promise of restoration (vv. 17-21). He perceives it as the divine response to the priestly prayer at 2.17; this may be so, though there is little evidence for so precise an analysis. We shall here be more concerned with the internal details of this chapter, where his analysis is certainly valuable. To a large extent it corresponds with the paragraph divisions in NRSV.

It soon becomes clear that the promise to **all flesh** of 2.28 (3.1) is not to be regarded as straightforward universalism. The tension between Israel and the nations remains an acute one. It is now very specifically **the fortunes of Judah and Jerusalem** that are to be **restored**. As in Amos 9.14 an interesting element in the history of interpretation is provided by the expression *'āšub šᵉbut*. Older translations, notably KJV, rendered this as 'bring again the captivity', and with such an understanding, it was natural to see here an expression of hope for a return of the community from exile. Modern scholars seem, however, to be unanimous in agreeing that a rendering such as 'restore the fortunes' is more appropriate.

3.2 (4.2). The picture presented in this verse might seem to invite us to ask geographical questions, to try to find out where on a map **the valley of Jehoshaphat** might be located. But virtually all recent commentators have recognized that such questions would be misguided. Allen is in general perhaps more inclined than most to seek a literal meaning in the text, but he recognizes that this is 'a theological symbol rather than a topographical identification' (Allen 1976: 109). It is therefore more appropriate to look for literary links than for otherwise unknown geographical locations.

The theme of **the valley** in which enemy forces are overthrown is a recurring one (Zech. 14.2-4), and this is the first occurrence of what will prove to be a marked characteristic of this chapter; the reuse of existing material from other prophetic texts. **Jehoshaphat** is of course a well-known proper name, particularly that of a ninth-century king of Judah. The account of his reign in 1–2 Kings is somewhat overshadowed by the attention paid to his northern contemporary Ahab, particularly in the Elijah stories, but he comes into his own in 2 Chronicles 17–20. Commentators on Chronicles are sharply divided as to whether the restructuring of the judicial system attributed to Jehoshaphat in 2 Chron. 19.4-11 has a historical basis, or is to be understood as inspired by the appropriateness of his name: 'Yahweh judges'. Certainly here it seems as if it is the significance of the name that is important. Part of this point is almost inevitably lost in any translation, but the Hebrew brings out the wordplay very strongly with two words based on the *šapaṭ* root following one another: *'el-'emeq yᵉhošapat wᵉnišpatti*.

The last part of the verse appears to be a prose elaboration with its use of the relative word *'ašer* and the accusative marker *'eth*, neither of which is usual in poetry. In addition, the judgment on the **nations** is because they have scattered Israel **among the nations**. The repetition of 'nations' (*goyim*) is as awkward in Hebrew as it is in English.

Elsewhere in the prophetic writings when other nations had brought about the scattering of Israel and the taking of the land, this was regarded as the carrying out of God's own decree; the role of Nebuchadnezzar in Jeremiah 27 is perhaps the most obvious example of this theme. Here such action is part of the accusation against the nations. We should be wrong to look for rigid consistency in religious literature of this kind.

3.3 (4.3). The accusation continues with the curious charge that the nations have **cast lots for my people**. The expression is found in two other passages in the Minor Prophets. Nahum 3.10 refers to the fate of the people of Thebes, in Egypt, and may not be relevant here, but at Obadiah 11 the reference is to foreign soldiers casting lots for Jerusalem, and it seems likely that this passage is an application of Obadiah, a text with which we have already noticed links; others will emerge later in this chapter (e.g. at v. 17). (Thus Bergler 1988: 305.)

The condemnations in the last part of the verse are clearly poetic once more, but their reference is not clear. It may be that some sexual practice is being condemned, but if so the allusion is a very oblique one. The last word in the Hebrew text, **and drunk it down**, is also curious; for what other purpose would one buy wine? Perhaps we should see a note of contempt, that the prophet's enemies could regard human beings as no more important than a mere drink (thus Crenshaw 1995: 177), but this may reflect modern liberal values rather than the world of Hebrew prophetism. It is perhaps not surprising that BHS should detect a rather prosaic addition here. Bergler (1988: 306) claims to see here a further link with Obadiah, this time to the drinking on the holy mountain mentioned in Obadiah 16. It may be right to see a link here, but it is more tenuous than many of the other ties.

3.4 (4.4). Following the general condemnation of 'all the nations' we now find a more specific accusation directed against **Tyre and Sidon, and all the regions of Philistia**. Many scholars have seen 3.4-8 (MT 4.4-8) as a distinct prose section, added at a later period to make more precise the general charges of the preceding verses (Prinsloo 1985: 106-110 summarizes the arguments used). Such a discussion reflects the assumptions of source-critical study; it may indeed be true that the basic material has been developed, but it seems better to confine ourselves to the book in the form in which it has been brought together.

Within these verses the charge is introduced by $w^e gam$, printed on a separate line in BHS and clearly intended as introducing a new or more specific point. It is not rendered by NRSV, but we might say 'What is more'. The exact force of the question is disputed. NRSV 's **What are you to me** might imply that Yahweh has no concern for these nations, but a better understanding may be that proposed by Wolff: 'What have you done to me?', probably a legal phrase to introduce a series of charges (Wolff 1977: 77).

Several scholars have detected a symmetrical pattern in vv. 4-8, described by Nogalski (1993b: 29) as a picture of 'poetic justice which goes full circle'. The 'circle' forms both a theological and a geographical pattern. Links with two other prophetic contexts have been proposed for the series of loaded questions that now follows. On the one hand Nogalski argues that the references to Tyre and the regions of Philistia serve as catchwords providing a link forward to the oracles against foreign nations at the beginning of Amos (1.8-9). More specifically the word $g^e mul$ ('recompense'), found three times in this verse (NRSV translates as a verb, **paying me back/turn back**) offers a further link with Obadiah, where at v. 15 we find 'your deeds ($g^e mulka$) shall return on your own head'. Seybold (1972: 115) thought in terms of a word-play on the different senses of g-m-l, but the link with Obadiah seems more plausible. It would certainly make good sense to see in our passage a reapplication of the earlier assertion.

At the end of the verse as translated in English the repetition of the two adverbs *qal* and *mᵉhērāh*, which are virtual synonyms, **swiftly and speedily**, serves to emphasize that there can be no escaping from the fate spelt out.

3.5 (4.5). The prose character of this section is brought out by the fact that this verse begins with the relative word *'ašer*, rarely found in poetry. Its theme is one which recurs in the Hebrew Bible, sometimes giving rather contradictory effects. On the one hand emphasis is placed upon the effrontery of the enemy in taking away the **rich treasures** devoted to Yahweh's worship and putting them to common use. This point is brought out here, and Belshazzar's feast in Daniel 5 is the classic illustration of this reading. But on the other hand it was also important to stress the continuity in worship that the temple vessels ensured, and so we find other passages where their wonderful preservation is emphasized (Ezra 1). (Ackroyd 1987 does not refer to our present passage, but it illustrates his basic theme.)

3.6 (4.6). This is one of the rather few verses in Joel where it seems as if a sociological approach may usefully be adopted. The **Greeks** referred to here were presumably slave-traders. It would be unwise to make deductions about the date of the text from such a reference, for activities of this kind will have continued over a long period. In any case the theme is introduced here, partly in order to provide the context for its reversal in v. 8, partly because it is in a more general sense appropriate for the 'day of judgment' language which pervades this section.

3.7 (4.7). Nogalski's analysis requires that this verse be taken with what precedes, but we should also notice that there is a significant shift forward in thought. The accusations are over; now we are beginning to hear the verdict. The *gᵉmul* theme of v. 4 emerges once again; the warning goes out that **I will turn your deeds back upon your own heads**. The picture of 'all flesh' receiving the divine spirit (2.28) has been rather drastically modified.

3.8 (4.8). The process of reversal, already hinted at in v. 7 with its use of the *gᵉmul* theme, is now taken a stage further. Just as Judah's enemies had sold them as slaves (v. 6), now God **will sell your sons and daughters**. We might be tempted to suppose that the innate cruelty of such action is increased by it being done to 'sons and daughters', with a picture in our minds of young and innocent children. The truth is probably more prosaic, with 'sons and daughters' simply a way of referring to the inhabitants of a place. The **people of Judah**, no longer themselves under threat of slavery, will heighten the indignity imposed upon their enemies by selling them on **to the Sabeans, a nation far away**. Commentators have differed as to whether we should see in this a reference to two distinct peoples (so Rudolph) or as one, the Sabeans being regarded as the distant nation (so Allen). In any case it may be better to see a poetic flight of fancy rather than an ethnic issue. The 'Sabeans' are probably referred to in Ps. 72.10 (NRSV 'kings of Sheba'), though the elaborate alliteration of the Psalm verse at that point makes certain identification doubtful. The references at Isa. 45.14 and Job 1.14-15 are less obscure, and give us the picture of a distant people, known as traders and raiders. To be sold into slavery in their custody was not an enviable fate. The selling on of enemies envisaged here is not directly contradictory to any law in the Pentateuch, though it is scarcely consonant with the kind of practice that is there enjoined.

3.9 (4.9). This verse is clearly poetry, by comparison with the rhythmic prose which has preceded it. We are transported back to the valley of judgment with a series of imperatives reminiscent of the book of Nahum. MT breaks the sequence of imperatives with the last two (**draw near, come up**) being ordinary finite verbs. BHS wishes to emend them to imperatives, but this may be imposing upon the text the idiom of style expected by modern scholars. This was certainly the case with NEB, which proposed a most complicated rearrangement of vv. 9-12. REB has restored the order of MT, and the only commentary that I know to be based specifically on NEB (Watts 1975) took no notice of the rearrangement in its comments. In any case, in accordance with the 'oracles against the nations' of many prophetic collections, this is a message which is to be proclaimed **among the nations**.

For the modern reader a very embarrassing message it is. The translation of RSV/NRSV, **prepare war**, can only be regarded as a cop-out; the margin makes it clear that the command is to 'sanctify war'. War was a fact of life in the ancient world, and the biblical text is not exempt from that generalization. In the New Testament, Jesus takes warfare for granted (e.g. Lk. 14.31-32). Our passage, however, goes beyond that. Here we have the language of 'holy war'. Just as Yahweh himself is pictured as a 'warrior' (Exod. 15.3), so it is entirely acceptable to regard warfare waged on Yahweh's behalf as holy.

3.10 (4.10). There now follows one of the most striking examples of reuse of prophetic material found in Joel. Isaiah 2.4 and Mic. 4.3 contain the well-known announcement that

> in days to come
> they shall beat their swords into ploughshares,
> and their spears into pruning hooks.'

Here three of the four operative words are repeated. *'et*, 'blade', or traditionally 'ploughshare', *ḥereb*, 'sword' and *mazmerah*, 'pruning-knife' are found both here and in Isaiah and Micah. The fourth word differs: *ḥānit* in Isaiah and Micah, *romaḥ* here. Though it is possible that two slightly different types of spear are envisaged, it seems unlikely that we should look to the logistics of warfare as explaining the change. It may be that this change of vocabulary is a conscious way of indicating the change of message. For it is obvious enough that the pacific sense of the Isaiah/Micah passage has been transformed (Coggins 1996: 77-78). We are moving from the theme of warfare waged as liberation from specific oppressors to the kind of picture of warfare against all forms of tyranny found in the apocalypses. This impression is strengthened by the conclusion of the verse: even **the weakling** (*ḥallaš*, not elsewhere used as a noun) will be given the strength of **a warrior**.

3.11 (4.11). Imperatives follow, but our appreciation of them is hindered by uncertainty as to their meaning, particularly of the first of them: *'ušu*, a word found only here in the Hebrew Bible. BDB 736a, following the warning note 'si vera l.' ('if this is the true reading'), proposed 'lend aid', and was able to offer some mediaeval Jewish understanding in support. This suggestion no doubt owed much to S.R. Driver, and it was followed up by his son, Sir Godfrey Driver, who was very influential in proposing solutions to difficult problems for the NEB. There we find 'Rally to each other's help'. But this interpretation was part of that drastic reordering of vv. 9-12 that we have already noted, and in any case this understanding does not seem especially appropriate in context. REB has therefore reverted to the usual ordering of verses, and renders our verb as 'muster'. BHS takes the text to be corrupt, and proposes reading either *'uru*, 'awake' or *ḥōšû* 'make haste', but these suggestions are no more than speculation.

Bergler draws attention to the similarity between this verse and Jer. 49.13-14 (Bergler 1988: 313-16). The initial verb is different, so that the parallel passage sheds no light on that problem, but each is a summons to war.

It is clear that the verb in the next clause (*wᵉniqbaṣû* in MT) has the

sense of gathering. In its MT form it is a finite verb, but BHS proposes
emending to *hiqqabᵉṣu*, the imperative, and whether or not the textual
emendation is accepted an imperative sense seems to be demanded by
the context. (Thus NRSV without note.)

The textual difficulties of the verse have not yet all been noted, however, for the last clause has been very variously understood. Barthélemy
(1992: 638-40) devotes a detailed note to this clause. Characteristically,
after a careful consideration of various proposed emendations he and
his committee vote to retain the MT, taking *šammāh*, **there**, with what
follows rather than with what precedes (as in NRSV) and proposes a
translation very similar to NRSV's **Bring down your warriors, O
Lord**. The War Scroll from Qumran contains similar phraseology,
applied there to the theme of angelic warriors. Many commentators,
however, have found this reading unacceptable. Allen, for example,
feels that the form of a prayer is inappropriate here, and claims to follow the Greek in rendering 'Let the timid man become a hero', that is, a
reversion to the theme already found at the end of v. 10.

Certainty here is impossible, but, whatever the details we are clearly
in the realm of a war which has gone beyond the scope of ordinary
human conflict.

3.12 (4.12). This verse clearly forms an inclusio with v. 2. Here as
there the **nations** are to be brought to judgment in **the valley of
Jehoshaphat**. The rendering of NRSV, **neighbouring nations**, though
probably intended to avoid the ambiguous phrase 'nations round about'
found in RSV and REB, may not convey the appropriate sense. Such a
wording makes it sound as if only the traditional rivals of Israel—
Edom, Moab and so on—are intended; this judgment is surely on a
more universal scale than that. The identical phrase, *kol haggōyim
missābib*, occurred in v. 11, where it was rendered 'all you nations all
around', and that conveyed the sense better. It is interesting also to note
that there is a further link here with Micah 4. In v. 10 we saw the reuse
of the 'swords into ploughshares' theme of Mic. 4.3; here the gathering
of the nations offers links with Mic. 4.12 where the assembly of the
nations brings unexpected judgment upon them.

3.13 (4.13). Once again imperatives follow. The picture is a familiar
one in a description of judgment; it is likened to a **harvest**. The third of
the imperatives, *rᵉdu*, was taken by older versions as coming from the
common verb *yārad*, 'to go down': hence AV 'get you down'. But most
recent interpreters and translators have proposed that the verb is

actually *rādāh*, 'to tread' (so e.g. KBL 874), and this offers a more
natural sense here. **The vats overflow** is a phrase already found at 2.24,
but the repetition is surely ironic. In the earlier verse the harvest had
been a symbol of the blessing which God's people might anticipate;
here it is a devastating judgment to be brought on the nations because
their wickedness is great.

3.14 (4.14). *h^{a}monim*, the word translated **multitudes**, refers not only
to the size of the crowds, but also to the uproar they cause. (BDB 242a
offers as meanings: 'sound, murmur, roar, crowd, abundance'.) It is
likely that there is an allusion here to Isa. 13.4 (' a tumult [*h^{a}mōn*] upon
the mountains'. This comes in a passage which we have already seen to
be reflected in Joel (cf. 1.15 with Isa. 13.6). The solemnity of the occasion is reflected by repetition, both of the first word, and of the phrase
b^{e}emeq haḥārūṣ, **in the valley of decision**. *ḥārūṣ*, 'decision' is found in
this form only here in the Hebrew Bible, but the verb from which it is
derived is a well-known one, and it brings out clearly the theme of
judgment as a time of decision.

3.15 (4.15). Apocalyptic language in general, and that relating to the
day of the Lord in particular, often uses imagery picturing the disruption of the heavenly bodies; the book of Revelation, in the New
Testament, is particularly rich in this respect. But the words of this
verse have already been found at 2.10b, and there are also substantial
links with 2.31a (MT 3.4a), an indication of the editorial unity of our
book.

3.16 (4.16). This verse also alludes to 2.10, though this time in a
more indirect way. As in the earlier verse, **the heavens and the earth**
are to be disturbed, but a different verb (*rā'aš*) is here used to picture
the shaking. Perhaps more striking, however, is the identity with Amos
1.2 displayed by the first part of the verse. It is possible that we should
see in the phraseology here used dependence on, or borrowing from, the
Jerusalem cult-tradition. Jeremiah 25.30 is very close to the expression
found here, while Isa. 13.13 also makes use of the theme of heaven and
earth being 'shaken' (*rā'aš*). With regard to the Amos link, we might
note that, since that book displays very little other interest in Jerusalem,
it might be that 1.2 was incorporated in Amos at the point when its
material was brought together at Jerusalem. However that may be, it
does seem as if a conscious linkage was intended at the editorial stage
between Joel and Amos, and recent interest in the putting together of
the 'Book of the Twelve' (i.e. the 'Minor Prophets') has fastened on

this point (Bergler 1988: 144-45).

In its present context, however, this verse is more than a quotation. It also marks the beginning of the 'happy ending' of the book as a whole. The immediately preceding verses have stressed the imminence and terrifying nature of the judgment that other nations might expect. Here the correlative point is made that **the Lord is a refuge for his people**. This picture of a 'refuge' (*maḥᵃseh*) is found frequently in the Psalms (eleven examples are listed by BDB 340b, the first being Ps. 14.6). The idea of a **stronghold** (*ma'oz*) is very close to that of a refuge, and this description of the divine protection is also found in the Psalms (four times, beginning at 27.1). Here once again it is certainly possible to see links with the Jerusalem cult tradition.

3.17 (4.17). These links are carried forward very strongly in this verse. Indeed, in the last six verses of the book, **Zion** and **Jerusalem** are used together in synonymous parallelism three times. Again there are links within the 'Book of the Twelve', this time most obviously with Obadiah 17, where the holy mountain, Zion, is pictured as a refuge. Williamson (*ISBE*, II, 1078) also suggested links between this verse and Ezek. 36.11, but though the theme of the restoration of Zion is common to both passages, it is not so easy to detect specific inter-textual allusions here.

A topic frequently mentioned in the later prophetic texts is that of aliens and their relation to the Jerusalem community. One approach is to claim that the unique status of Jerusalem and its worship will be demonstrated by the eagerness of foreigners to go there, as it were on pilgrimage (Isa. 60.1-7; Zech. 8.20-23; 14.16-19). A different understanding is found here and in such passages as Isa. 52.1-2.

3.18 (4.18). This long verse serves a double function. On the one hand it forms an *inclusio* with 1.5. There, at the beginning of the book, the lack of **sweet wine** had been one of the deprivations that the community had had to face after the depradations of the locusts. Here it will be so abundant that the very **mountains shall drip sweet wine**.

That expression introduces us to the other function of this verse; it offers another link with Amos, this time the end of that book (9.13) (the two passages are identical except that they use different forms of the verb *nāṭap*, 'drip'). It seems clear that one of the purposes of the editors of Joel was to place the collection securely within the total context of the 'Book of the Twelve'.

It is possible that the reference to **the streambeds of Judah** flowing

with water is a deliberate contrast with 1.20, where the same word
(*'ᵃpiqe*; NRSV 'watercourses') had been used as part of the description
of the desolation that is here pictured as being reversed. The remainder
of the verse develops the imagery in a manner reminiscent of Ezekiel
47. **The Wadi Shittim** may be a specific place-name, as is implied by
NRSV, but it is also possible that it is a more general reference to aca-
cias, which are known for growing in the driest places. Even they will
be well-watered.

    3.19-20 (4.19-20). Nationalistic fervour of an unattractive kind intro-
duces the last paragraph of the book. Delight in Judah's fertility is to be
enhanced by the vision of the **desolation** of her enemies. **Egypt** and
Edom might seem to be rather an unusual pairing, one a long-lasting
great empire, the other one of the small neighbour states of Judah. They
are also treated together in Deut. 23.7-8, but there they are singled out
for comparatively favourable treatment, by comparison with the
Ammonites and Moabites. Here, by contrast, they are strongly condemned. Various explanations have been put forward for this juxtaposition of Egypt and Edom, usefully summarized by Dicou (1994),
esp. p. 81. Some scholars have supposed that the reference is primarily
historical. Either the way in which these nations left Judah to its fate at
the hands of Nebuchadnezzar of Babylon, or some otherwise unknown
later episode, would provide the context. An explanation of this type
cannot be ruled out, but our ignorance of the date of Joel make it very
speculative. In any case it seems unlikely that we should be able to
trace specific historical allusions in visionary literature of this type.

    A different explanation was put forward by Bergler (1988: 327-33).
For him this is in effect the climax of a major theme running throughout
the book: a new Exodus-typology. Egypt and Edom are typical enemies
whose power will be overthrown in the day of Yahweh. As we have
seen already, this argument may be weakened by the fact that in
Deuteronomy these nations are regarded less unfavourably than others.
We should also notice that there are thematic links between this part of
Joel and the 'day of the Lord' picture in Obadiah 15–22.

    One small textual point in this first part of the verse may be noted,
mainly to show how fashions in textual criticism have changed. In the
Hebrew the expression *šᵉmāmāh tihyeh* (**shall become a desolation**) is
found twice, in reference to both Egypt and Edom. BHS thought that
one of these words should be deleted in its second occurrence, on
grounds of metrical overloading. The more recent custom is to admit

our uncertainties as to metrical requirements in Hebrew poetry and to see in this repetition a deliberate dramatic emphasis.

The remainder of this verse and v. 20 spell out the contrast between the fate of these violent nations and the restoration promised to Judah. Here, as often in the Hebrew Bible, we find **Judah** and **Jerusalem** in parallel. It is difficult to know whether this is intended as synonymous parallelism, two ways of referring to the same community, or whether a sense still remains of the two entities being distinct. It is widely held that in Isaiah, for example, a distinction between Judah and Jerusalem is intended; whether that is also the case here is less obvious.

3.21 (4.21). The final verse of the book presents another textual difficulty. BHS has a short way with the problem, suggesting that the whole verse may be a later addition. But that seems only to compound the difficulty; later additions are most naturally understood as attempts to resolve an ambiguity, whereas here such an addition would itself be the cause of the ambiguity. Read literally (cf. NRSV margin) we have 'I will make their blood innocent which I have not made innocent'.

It is possible to make sense of this, by supposing that the point is that God will no longer punish his people in the way that he had done in the past. This was the solution adopted almost a century ago by Driver (1915: 80), and still advocated by Barthélemy (1992: 641). This may be right, but one has the uneasy feeling that such a solution is partly based on the desire to uphold the MT come what may. An obvious possible emendation is to suppose that instead of the verb *nāqāh* which underlies the MT, the first verb should be *nāqam*, similar in form but different in meaning. The basic sense of *nāqāh* is 'to be innocent', whereas *nāqam* means 'to take vengeance'. It is possible that the LXX translation read two different verbs here, ἐκδικησω and ἀθοωσω, which could argue for the use of *nāqam* in the first instance, *nāqāh* in the second. This is the reasoning behind NRSV : **I will avenge their blood, and I will not clear the guilty**. Another possibility, favoured by Allen (1976: 117), who also provides a list of other proposals which have been made, is that the first clause should be understood as a question: 'And shall I leave their bloodshed unpunished? I will not.' It is probably wise to acknowledge our uncertainty as to how best to understand this line, and it is scarcely possible here to explore the inherent moral difficulty involved in proclaiming a God of vengeance. Few of the commentators studied seem to have found this a problem.

In any case there can be no doubt about what follows: the book ends with the triumphant repetition of the claim made in v. 17, that Yahweh dwells in Zion. Here in this final phrase we see both of the themes we have been pursuing brought once again to the fore. On the one hand this is the language we should expect if we are to picture Joel as based on the Jerusalem cult; on the other hand it looks as if an element of inner-biblical exegesis may be detected in this claim with its strong reminiscence of Ezek. 43.7.

BIBLIOGRAPHY

Ackroyd, P.R
1987   'The Temple Vessels: A Continuity Theme', in *idem, Studies in the Religious Tradition of the Old Testament* (London: SCM Press): 46-60.

Ahlstrom, G.W.
1971   *Joel and the Temple Cult of Jerusalem* (VTSup, 21; Leiden: E.J. Brill).

Allen, L.C.
1976   *The Books of Joel, Obadiah, Jonah and Micah* (NICOT; Grand Rapids, MI: Eerdmans).

Alter, R.
1990   *The Art of Biblical Poetry* (Edinburgh: T. & T. Clark).

Archer, G.L., Jr
1985   *A Survey of Old Testament Introduction* (Chicago: Moody Press, 2nd edn, 1985 [1974]).

Barthélemy, D.
1992   *Critique textuelle de l'Ancien Testament. III. Ézéchiel, Daniel et les 12 Prophètes* (OBO 50.3; Fribourg Suisse: Editions Universitaires; Göttingen: Vandenhoeck & Ruprecht).

Bergler , S.
1988   *Joel als Schriftinterpret* (BEATAJ, 16; Frankfurt: Peter Lang).

Bewer, J.A.
1912   'Joel', in J.M. Powis Smith, W.H. Ward and Bewer, *A Critical and Exegetical Commentary on Micah, Zephaniah, Nahum, Habakkuk, Obadiah and Joel* (ICC; Edinburgh: T.& T. Clark).

Bic, M.
1960   *Das Buch Joel* (Berlin: Evangelische Verlagsanstalt) [Not available to me; the references to this work are based on comments made by other scholars.]

Bolin, T.M.
1997   *Freedom beyond Forgiveness: The Book of Jonah Re-examined* (JSOTSup, 236; Sheffield: Sheffield Academic Press).

Childs, B.S.
1979   *Introduction to the Old Testament as Scripture* (London: SCM Press).

Coggins, R.J.
1982   'An Alternative Prophetic Tradition?', in R.J. Coggins, A. Phillips and M. Knibb (eds.), *Israel's Prophetic Tradition: Essays in Honour of Peter R. Ackroyd* (Cambridge: Cambridge University Press): 77-94.

1996   'Interbiblical Quotations in Joel', in J. Barton and D.J. Reimer (eds.), *After the Exile: Essays in Honour of Rex Mason* (Macon, GA; Mercer University Press): 75-84.

66 JOEL AND AMOS

Conrad, E.W.
1985   *Fear not, Warrior: A Study of 'al tira' Pericopes in the Hebrew Scriptures* (Atlanta, GA: Scholars Press).
Cook, S.L.
1995   *Prophecy and Apocalypticism: The Post-Exilic Social Setting* (Minneapolis: Fortress Press).
Crenshaw, J.L.
1995   *Joel* (AB 24C; Doubleday: New York).
Delcor, M.
1961   *Les petites prophètes* (La Sainte Bible, 8.1; Paris: Letouzey & Ané).
Dicou, B.
1994   *Edom, Israel's Brother and Antagonist: The Role of Edom in Biblical Prophecy and Story* (JSOTSup, 169; Sheffield: Sheffield Academic Press).
Driver, S.R.
1915   *The Books of Joel and Amos* (Cambridge Bible for Schools and Colleges; Cambridge: Cambridge University Press, 2nd edn, 1915 [1897]).
Fishbane, M.
1985   *Biblical Interpretation in Ancient Israel* (Oxford: Clarendon Press).
Hanson, P.D.
1979   *The Dawn of Apocalyptic: The Historical and Sociological Roots of Jewish Apocalyptic Eschatology* (Philadelphia: Fortress Press, 2nd edn).
Hubbard, D.A.
1989   *Joel and Amos* (TOTC; Leicester: IVP).
Hvidberg, F.F.
1962   *Weeping and Laughter in the Old Testament* (ET; Leiden: E.J. Brill [1938]).
Kapelrud, A.S.
1948   *Joel Studies* (Uppsala: Almqvist & Wiksell).
Koch, K.
1982   *The Prophets. I. The Assyrian Period* (London: SCM Press).
Loretz, O.
1986   *Regenritual und Jahwetag im Joelbuch* (Ugaritisch-Biblische Literatur, 4; Athenberge: CIS Verlag).
Mason, R.
1994   *Zephaniah Habakkuk Joel* (OTG; Sheffield: Sheffield Academic Press).
Nogalski, J.
1993a   *Literary Precursors to the Book of the Twelve* (BZAW, 217; Berlin: W. de Gruyter).
1993b   *Redactional Processes in the Book of the Twelve* (BZAW, 218; Berlin: W. de Gruyter).
Plöger, O.
1968   *Theocracy and Eschatology* (trans. S. Rudman; Oxford: Basil Blackwell; original German edition, 1959).
Prinsloo, W.S.
1985   *The Theology of the Book of Joel* (BZAW, 163; Berlin: W. de Gruyter).
Redditt, P.L.
1986   'The Book of Joel and Peripheral Prophecy', *CBQ* 48 (1986): 225-40.

Roth, C.
 1963 'The Teacher of Righteousness and the Prophecy of Joel', *VT* 13.1
  (1963): 91-95.
Rudolph, W.
 1971 *Joel, Amos, Obadja, Jona* (KAT XIII, 2; Gütersloh: Gerd Mohn).
Schmidt, W.H.
 1995 *Einführung in das Alte Testament* (5 erweiterte Auflage; Berlin: W. de
  Gruyter).
Seybold, K.
 1972 'Zwei Bemerkungen zu *gml/gmol*', *VT* 12.1: 112-17.
Soggin, J.A.
 1989 *Introduction to the Old Testament* (London: SCM Press, 3rd edn).
Stephenson , F.R.
 1969 'The Date of the Book of Joel', *VT* 19.2 (1969): 224-29.
Thompson, J.A.
 1974 'The Date of Joel', in H.N. Bream, R.D. Heim and C.A. Moore (eds.), *A
  Light unto my Path: Old Testament Studies in Honor of Jacob M. Myers*
  (Philadelphia: Temple University Press): 453-64.
Watts, J.D.W.
 1975 *The Books of Joel, Obadiah, Jonah, Nahum, Habakkuk and Zephaniah*
  (CBC; Cambridge: Cambridge University Press).
Wolff, H.W.
 1977 *Joel and Amos* (Hermeneia; Philadelphia: Fortress Press). (ET of *Joel und
  Amos* (BKAT, 14.2; Neukirchen–Vluyn: Neukirchner Verlag, 2nd edn,
  1975).

COMMENTARY
ON AMOS

AMOS

1. WHAT ARE WE STUDYING?

It has been a very general assumption among commentators on almost every book of the Hebrew Bible during the last 200 years that the reader is, or wishes to be treated as, an historian. It has seemed essential to explore the historical circumstances in which the book came together; to isolate (and then often virtually ignore) particular verses or more extended sections that probably originated from a different background; to explore what could be known about the author in his historical context. A commentary that simply invited the reader to engage with, say, a prophetic book, for itself, without regard to its alleged historical setting, would be dismissed from serious consideration as unscholarly: 'devotional' or 'edifying' would be typical of the epithets applied to such a work. One of the reasons for the relative neglect of the wisdom writings was that they did not lend themselves readily to such an history-based approach.

Nowhere has this 'life and times' approach been more prevalent than with books such as Amos. The book of Amos has been bracketed together with Hosea, Micah and Isaiah 1–39, and they are then collectively described as 'the eighth-century prophets'. Important assumptions are already built into such a description. We are being invited to read these books as illuminated by, and as contributing to, our knowledge of a specific historical period. Any material that seems not to fit into that setting is labelled with derogatory terms such as 'secondary' or 'not original'. In particular, interest quickly shifts from the book to the alleged author. The underlying 'personality' of the prophet moves to the centre of the stage.

The point can be illustrated by a brief quotation from one of the most influential popular studies of the Hebrew Bible written in the last 60 years: *Personalities of the Old Testament*, by Fleming James. Written in a lively and engaging style, it was once said to have done more to help students pass their Old Testament examinations than any other book (including of course the Bible itself). Here he is on Amos:

> Leaving his sheep in the tangled hills and valleys of Judah he strode
> northward twenty-five miles till he reached Bethel, the religious centre of
> Israel. We may picture him in his rough herdsman's dress coming fresh
> from awful intercourse with deity into the crowded court of Bethel's
> famous sanctuary (James 1939: 215-16).

We should not ask what happened to the unfortunate sheep left behind
in Judah. We are invited here to concentrate on the messenger as the
key to the message; indeed James specifically stated that 'the sole
source for the study of Amos is the Book of Amos' (211). That is to
say, the primary topic of concern when we look at this piece of literature, is the individual for whom it is named, rather than the book itself.
Here with a vengeance is the romantic view of history as essentially
shaped by the actions and words of great men. (And of course it is
almost always men rather than women who are at the centre of attention.)

Among more recent scholars, even among those who continue to see
the figure of Amos himself as the central concern, a very different evaluation has become usual. Blenkinsopp (1996: 79), for example, suggests
that Amos may appropriately be described as a 'dissident intellectual'.
He notes the wide interest in and knowledge of the affairs of surrounding nations shown in the book, together with a profound knowledge of Israel's own sacral traditions, and great poetic skill. All this is a
long way from James's colourful portrayal, but the focus of attention is
still the figure of Amos himself.

One consequence of such a view as that of Blenkinsopp would be
that it implies that there was a great difference between Amos and any
of the prophetic figures whose activity is described in the books of
Samuel and Kings. With Elijah, for example, 'dissident' might be an
appropriate epithet, but he is scarcely presented as an intellectual!
There has been much dispute as to the relation between Amos and such
earlier figures as Nathan, Ahijah, Elijah and Elisha. At first glance they
seem very different, since the earlier figures are presented essentially as
'doers', involved in the activity of the royal court, whereas the 'eighth
century prophets' were essentially speakers, uttering oracles in the
name of Yahweh. From the very outset our collection is described as
'The words of Amos' (1.1). Scholarly opinion has long been sharply
divided on the relation between the two types of figure. Some have
stressed the fact that they were all described as prophets, and seen the
one as a natural development from the other. An alternative view has

been to emphasize the differences, at times making great claims for the
'eighth century prophets' as the discoverers of ethical monotheism.

We shall not look in detail here at the arguments put forward in this
dispute, for it assumes that there is a constant given factor; that we
know precisely who 'the prophets' were during the monarchical period,
what role they played in society and so on. This view has come to be
challenged, for example by the work of Auld, who has stressed that we
can only see the prophets 'through the looking glass' (Auld 1983). He
maintains that our perception of prophets and prophecy is mediated to
us through the work of later, particularly deuteronomistic, editors. This
has been an important contribution to a development that was already
taking place: the fact that much recent study has come to concentrate
more on the book than on the figure of Amos himself,

This development needs to be understood in the context of broader
changes of emphasis in the study of the Hebrew Bible in recent years.
In part this is simply a reflection of changing interests in the study of
texts. 'Authors', real or implied, and their concerns, have gone out of
fashion. Literary critics who disagree about other issues have been at
one in insisting that the primary focus of our attention must be the text
that has been handed down to us. As far as the Hebrew Bible is concerned, this different emphasis has been especially marked with the
narrative material, but it has also affected approaches to its prophetic
literature. It has been reinforced by increasing scepticism about what
can really be known of either the life or the times of many of the
prophets, and this is a point to which we shall need to return. Before
doing so, however, it may be relevant to note some other contributory
factors in this change of emphasis.

The first arises simply from the fact that Amos is 'Scripture' for
Jewish and Christian believers. What is venerated in these religious
communities is the text. If such a reading of the Prophets lends itself to
such epithets as 'devotional' or 'edifying', then so be it, though it is
worth noting that, appropriate as those epithets may be for some parts
of the Bible they would not readily spring to mind as descriptions of
Amos. Nevertheless, for believers within Judaism or Christianity these
are holy texts. The personalities of the individuals mentioned in them
may be of interest, may in some cases even rank as examples to be followed. But the text is primary. It forms part of a 'canon' of Scripture,
and is to be studied in that context.

In addition to this we may observe in passing that there is a certain irony in the attention paid to the Prophets in the prosperous West of our modern world. Many of the prophetic books, and Amos not least, are full of vigorous denunciations of the 'establishment' of their day. Modern commentators who are to all appearance part of today's thriving establishment often come out with unexpectedly radical, even Marxist, views, associating themselves with the sweeping condemnations that the book of Amos offers against the establishment of its day.

Again, we shall not be able to explore in detail in this volume the insights of 'liberation theology', but it is important to bear in mind that in parts of the world where believers have felt themselves to be part of a persecuted under-class, Amos has been greatly valued for the challenge it sets out to the existing structures of society and those who were prospering. Carroll R. 1992 has explored this theme in considerable detail, applying it to the situation of the church in Latin America. He is more ready than are many recent interpreters to see the influence of the prophet Amos himself in the final text, but his work provides a vivid reminder of the immediacy of a biblical text for a religious community that is seen and sees itself as 'outsiders'. In a shorter article he has offered a 'reading of the text of Amos as a possible means both to grapple with present Central American realities and to point to a new society beyond the violence' (Carroll R. 1995: 113). He stresses the part that 'official' religion plays in the main part of the book of Amos, and notes also its warlike associations. In his judgment these warlike links are deconstructed in the last few verses of the book, where, for example, the description of Yahweh as 'Lord God of Hosts', a warlike title, is no longer found. '9.11-15 offers a vision of peace and reconstruction' (Carroll R. 1995:121), and thereby provides hope for the deeply divided Christian community in Central America.

This is a most thought-provoking reading of the final form of the book, but it can hardly be regarded as typical. Most study of Amos has come from those who could in no sense be described as 'outsiders', and a second point arises from this. Much commentary on Amos has been of a remarkably moralising character. Readers have been invited to deplore the wickedness of those who are condemned in the book, and to see in their behaviour a major reason for the overrunning of Israel by the Assyrians a generation after the time of Amos. Such an interpretation of historical events would be greeted with scepticism by any serious historian, yet it is striking to find such views propagated by eminent scholars. (This is an issue to which we shall return below in our 'quest for the historical Amos'.)

Similarly, the strictures on human behaviour found in the book invite us to ask whether anything should be put forward in the defence of those so harshly attacked, and also to consider whether all of Amos's sweeping condemnations can be justified. Two recent studies may be cited as illustrating this latter point: Sanderson 1992 raises questions about Amos's attitude to women, and Clines 1995 offers a 'meta-commentary' on the book, inviting us to reflect on the indignant way in which conventional commentators often take up the words of Amos without adequate reflection.

The tendency therefore has increasingly been to approach Amos as a book, with less attention to the individual figure for whom it is named. Both for Amos and for other prophetic books, it is possible to discern that this development has taken two main forms, the results of which are very different. On the one hand, much recent biblical study has in effect been literary criticism, not in the older sense of source-analysis, but as an encounter with the different biblical books as pieces of litera-ture and an exploration of them at that level. On the other hand, another important recent development has been the attempt to place particular pieces of writing within the sociological structure of ancient Israel, and has recognized the tensions that existed between different groups. In this context is the book of Amos simply to be read as the good con-fronting the bad with their wickedness and warning of what its author took to be inevitable consequences? Or should we see the interplay of different social groups? We will consider the implications of this socio-logical approach first.

2. THE ORIGIN OF THE BOOK OF AMOS

If we are to look at the interplay of different social groups we need to have some idea of the background circumstances. Here some historical awareness is still essential. Amos is conventionally dated in the eighth century BCE. If we accept that dating we can say that among the small states in the area of Syria-Palestine there were two of special concern to the biblical writers: Israel and Judah. They were constantly at odds with one another, but were also aware of close ties that bound them together. Such ties were not confined to Israel and Judah; the state of Edom, East of the Jordan, was also described as a 'brother' (1.11). We find stories in the earlier part of the Hebrew Bible, especially in the book of Gen-esis, explaining the origin of these relationships (the 'tribes' of Israel;

Jacob and Esau [Edom] as brothers). Whether they are to be treated purely as stories, or whether they contain any nucleus of historical information, is a matter on which scholars are deeply divided.

Whatever answer is given to that question the great majority of commentators have supposed that Amos offers us reliable information on how these matters were perceived in the eighth century. Many popular writers and a significant number of more technical scholars have seen virtually the whole of Amos as the product of Amos himself, faithfully preserved by his disciples (thus Paul 1991). In any case there has been a widespread consensus which has accepted the greater part of the book as coming from the eighth century, with just a few passages thought to be later additions (possibly the oracles against Tyre and Edom, 1.9-12, and more probably that against Judah, 2.4-5; isolated verses such as 3.7 said to reflect a 'Deuteronomistic' viewpoint; the three Psalm-like passages in 4.13, 5.8-9 and 9.5-6; and above all the 'happy ending' in 9.8b, 11-15). These have been labelled as 'secondary'. Historical critical study has approached the book of Amos in the way that an art historian might approach a Renaissance masterpiece, cleaning away the traces of later additions, so that the original might be revealed in all its glory.

It is, however, very doubtful whether a prophetic book can be treated in this way. Those concerned to restore a Renaissance masterpiece will have a good idea of what the other paintings by the artist or his contemporaries are like. But we are embarrassingly short of clues as to what an eighth century BCE collection of prophetic oracles might have been like. Indeed, in Amos the only passages that could be taken as specifically referring to Israel in the eighth century are the introduction at 1.1, and the well-known prose episode in 7.10-17. The difficulty is that both of these passages have come to be added to the list of additions mantioned above. The introductory verse is seen as part of the editorial framework; the story in ch. 7 is told about Amos in terms so strikingly similar to stories told about other prophetic figures that its original reference to Amos must be doubted.

The attempt to find independent confirmation of the eighth-century setting of Amos has invited the question whether archaeological investigation has any light to shed on the matter. King (1988) is described as 'an archaeological commentary', and has some interesting light to shed on the archaeology of ancient Israel in general terms, but the eighth-century origin of Amos is there taken for granted, and archaeological material from that period is simply assumed to shed light on the book.

Though full of interesting material, King's work shows itself to come from a now much questioned standpoint when the introduction asserts that 'biblical archaeology is a biblical and not an archaeological discipline' (King 1988: 13). Archaeology therefore can scarcely be used to shed independent light on our question. In particular it is not possible to use archaeological evidence to establish detailed developments in social history. It has often been asserted that one of the problems of Amos's time was that the rich were increasing their wealth while the poor were falling into increasing destitution. It is possible that this is so, but the archaeology of the Iron Age is far from being precise enough to support such claims. In addition there is of course the inherent danger involved in using poetry (which is what Amos essentially is) to 'prove' external circumstances.

Our present concern, however, is somewhat different. We need to ask whether the book of Amos, as it has come down to us, reflects the situation of the eighth century BCE or is better understood as coming from what is commonly referred to as 'the Second Temple period', a time when the previously independent kingdoms had been overrun and become part of the larger empire of the day, and the focus of interest for the biblical tradition was on the religious group centred upon the restored Jerusalem temple. Even if we assume that there is more ancient material now incorporated within the book, it is misleading to suppose that the particular thrust of such material can be recovered from an essentially later composition.

An example may help to clarify these generalizations. It is clear that the book as it has come down to us is opposed to the current practice of cultic worship. 5.21-24 is the clearest and best-known of several passages in that sense. This and other material may have had a specific origin in disputes between different cultic centres in the eighth century. In the final form of the book, however, it is also possible that we should see in this and other prophetic passages opposed to cultic worship a concern 'central to the intellectual currents of Hellenism' (Thompson 1999: 69). Such a view is of course linked with Thompson's general thesis that the Hebrew Bible is a product of the Hellenistic age, but the basic point holds true, that detailed appraisal of social and religious customs must be seen in the context of the final shaping of the book. Since that context may have been either the Persian or even the Hellenistic periods, the fifth to the third century, we should be wise to admit our ignorance of the detailed social background of Amos. This invites us to look in more detail at the other approach mentioned above, exploring Amos first of all as a piece of literature in the form in which it has come down to us.

3. THE STRUCTURE OF THE BOOK

As has just been noted, we need to take with full seriousness the fact that later additions to a literary text are not simply additions that can be cleaned away so as to reveal the original. They decisively reshape the text. Thus, to make a very obvious point, Amos, in the only form in which we have it, is a book with a happy ending. The last few verses are not an excrescence to be removed, so that we get at the 'real Amos'; they are an integral part of the book, confounding our expectations in the manner of so much great literature.

We need here to bear in mind a point already alluded to. 'Literary criticism', as a term applied to study of the Hebrew Bible, has undergone a drastic change of meaning. Once it implied the analysis of the material into sources and the removal of later additions. In more recent scholarship, on the other hand, it has come to be understood as an evaluation of the work that we have before us in its final form. In that sense this is a book that explores the relation between God and his people, full of warnings that Israel cannot expect to escape the disasters that would befall the surrounding nations. The people's own behaviour would leave them with no excuses. Yet the book comes to a note of confidence that God's promises are such that ultimately peace and prosperity would be restored.

It is certainly possible to take a sceptical view of such a presentation, suggesting that it reflects the triumph of hope over experience, but the criteria that are brought to bear on the judgment of Amos are, on such a reading, *literary* criteria. It is in the context of a literary appreciation of the book that we should say something about its structure.

This has often constituted a problem for those who wished to emphasize the immediacy of the prophet's own words; the elegantly structured literary product seems to be a long way from the simple rough shepherd of the traditional picture. After two introductory verses, supplying links both with the historical outline offered in 2 Kings, and with the preceding book of Joel, we then have a series of oracles against the nations (1.3–2.16). The middle part of the book contains a series of oracles beginning 'Hear this word' or 'Alas for' (3.1–6.14). A series of five visions is found in chs. 7–9, interrupted by a narrative section in prose (7.10-15; its exact extent is disputed), which has traditionally been regarded as providing our only significant information about the figure of Amos himself, but may rather invite comparison with other similar stories elsewhere in the Hebrew Bible. This section also contains some more 'Hear this' material (8.4-14). Then, as we have already seen, the threats give place to the happy ending from 9.8b onward. There are minor details that do not fit neatly into this overall pattern, but the only significant additional element is the series of three hymnic passages (4.13; 5.8-9; 9.5-6), reminiscent of the Psalms in their praise of Yahweh as creator. Though at the moment separated from one another, they may originally have belonged together. Their present placing enables them to be seen as a kind of refrain, stressing the creative power of God which underlies the turbulence described in the remainder of the book.

4. THE QUEST FOR THE 'HISTORICAL AMOS'

In the first part of this commentary we have seen how little can be known about the individual figure of Joel. It has commonly been supposed that the situation with regard to Amos is very different. In fact, however, after the opening verse, as we have already noted, only one brief section in the book, in ch. 7, appears to give us any biographical information about Amos, and, as we shall see in the commentary at that point, the reliability of this as a historical source has come under considerable questioning.

Many commentators have taken it for granted that we have perfectly adequate knowledge of the individual figure of Amos. Dispute has for the most part been confined to his social status: was he a simple shepherd or someone from a 'higher' stratum of society? His home-town is said to have been Tekoa (1.1): was that the well-known southern place of that name or an otherwise unknown northern location, perhaps in Galilee (For the latter view see Koch 1982: 70)? Were his concerns primarily social or primarily cultic? Questions such as these have been at issue, with the underlying assumption that our basic knowledge of Amos was assured.

In recent years this assumption has been called into question. First of all, it is very curious that there is no cross-reference between the different 'eighth century prophets', all supposedly active within a few years of one another in the same quite small area. With the exception of Isaiah they are also unmentioned in 2 Kings. One way of resolving that difficulty is the suggestion that the prophetic books are to be read as a kind of more detailed supplement to the tale of disaster unfolded in the closing chapters of 2 Kings. But that still leaves the lack of cross-reference unexplained, and the suggestion has therefore been made that the 'colophons to the prophetic books (i.e. the introductory verses specifying their time of activity) represent later editing and are not necessarily accurate in dating' (World's Classics Bible: Additional Notes 372).

This is an important issue which warrants slightly fuller consideration. First of all, it seems very likely that there *was* an individual named Amos. The name has no obvious symbolic value or 'meaning'. No one else in the Hebrew Bible is given this name. The rabbinic idea that he was so called because he stuttered is ingenious but has no support in biblical Hebrew. (In English translations it looks as if the father of Isaiah, Amoz [Isa. 1.1] has a closely similar name, but in Hebrew both the initial and the closing letters of the two names are different: here *'amos*, in Isaiah *'amoṣ*).

The question of date is more difficult. We have seen already that no modern historian would regard the various disasters that befell Israel from the late eighth century onward as the inevitable consequence of its sinful behaviour, but such a view would have been much closer to the understanding of the compilers of the Hebrew Bible. God was believed to be in control of events. How then could such disasters have taken place? There must have been adequate cause in the wrong behaviour of his worshippers, and some form of warning must have been issued. As our book itself says, 'Surely the Lord God does nothing without revealing his secret to his servants the prophets' (Amos 3.7). In other words the compilers of the material will have taken it for granted that the words of doom found in Amos and the other prophetic collections must have been uttered as a kind of final warning before disaster struck.

If any understanding along these lines is correct it still leaves open the question of whether the compilers were right in their ascription of dating. Certainty is impossible; we are brought face-to-face once again with the tension between an historical and a literary approach to the book. If we assume that the references to various northern sanctuaries—Bethel and Samaria in particular—are to be taken as reference to specific places known to the author of these oracles, then it will be natural to assume that they must date from a time before the fall of the northern kingdom, Israel, in around 722 BCE, and the traditional dating for Amos, c. 750, would be approximately correct. If on the other hand

we see these references as essentially literary, tying in with other traditions relating to those places found in large parts of the Hebrew Bible,
then certainty about dating becomes impossible—and indeed, on such a
reading, not very important. We then read these texts as literary prod-
ucts without special concern for their precise historical setting. There
can be no 'right' answer to questions of this kind. It is important to
keep in mind that we are in the presence of an ancient text, from Syria-
Palestine in the first millennium BCE, for such an awareness will alert
us to the dangers of applying it too readily to completely different life-
situations. But where some readers will be anxious to know in as great
detail as possible the life-setting from which this text arose, others will
be content to receive it for its literary power, and for the way in which it
addresses the perceived follies of its day.

5. TEXT AND VERSIONS

This commentary is based upon the Hebrew Masoretic Text, normally
as understood by NRSV, upon which all English translations are based
unless the contrary is stated. The Hebrew is in general well-preserved,
and no major structural changes are required. The Greek translation
(LXX) has its own distinctive understanding, to which reference is made
as appropriate in the commentary, but by and large LXX and other
translations should be approached as texts in their own right rather than
as means to modify the existing Hebrew.

COMMENTARY

1.1. This prose introductory verse appears to offer us a good deal of information concerning the background of Amos, but it has been very variously understood. (In addition to the commentaries, Nogalski 1993a: 76-78 supplies a useful survey of different views that have been taken concerning this opening verse.) We have already noted in the introduction the view that prefatory matter of this kind in all the prophetic collections is a later editorial product, with little historical worth.

First of all, it is unexpected that what we are to find in the book is **the words of Amos**. Other apparently parallel introductions speak of 'the word of the Lord' (cf. Hos. 1.1; Mic. 1.1). The body of the book makes clear the editors' conviction that Amos was indeed the messenger of the Lord. It has been widely supposed that the original form of the introduction consisted of this phrase together with the final part of the verse, so that we should have 'The words of Amos during the two years before the earthquake'. The relative clauses in the middle of the verse would then be later elaborations. This is an attractive possibility, though it is not susceptible of proof.

The two relative clauses certainly seem clumsy. The relative particle *'ašer* introduces each of them, but apparently with two different referents: first Amos himself, then his words. This is the natural understanding of the Hebrew, though the LXX apparently took it differently, referring both clauses to the words, 'which happened' (οἱ ἐγενοντο). Though this reading has been defended as original, it is not a very persuasive argument, particularly as the following Greek word (νακκαριμ) is otherwise unknown. It certainly looks as if this introductory formula has undergone elaboration.

The name 'Amos' is not found elsewhere in the Hebrew Bible. As we have seen already, the name 'Amoz' which is that of the father of Isaiah, Isa. 1.1, is closer in its English form than it is in Hebrew. The same Greek form of the name is found in the list of Jesus' ancestors at Lk. 3.24, but no one to my knowledge has proposed identifying these characters. Much has been made of the description of Amos as being **among the shepherds of Tekoa**. As we have seen in the introduction the description of Amos as a shepherd has led to some rather fanciful reconstructions of his role. In particular he has been seen as the simple

unlettered countryman shocked by what he regarded as the excesses of
city life. Two obvious difficulties present themselves for such a reconstruction. First, the elegance and indeed sophistication of much of the
Hebrew seems strangely at odds with this picture of the simple rustic;
we should have to suppose that his words had undergone a very elaborate editorial process. Secondly, the term *nōqᵉdīm*, here translated
'shepherds', is elsewhere used (in the singular, of course) of a king,
Mesha of Moab, 2 Kgs 3.4, where NRSV has 'sheep breeder'. This in
turn has led to equally fanciful reconstructions in a contrary sense, of
Amos being a breeder of sheep for the sacrificial requirements of the
Jerusalem temple. It would be wise to admit our ignorance of the precise nuance conveyed by the description.

Amos is said to have come from **Tekoa**. This is a placename found
several times in the Hebrew Bible (e.g. 2 Sam. 23.26), and is usually
identified with a site some ten miles south of Jerusalem, which still
retains the name Hirbet Tequ. This area would be possible for sheep-
breeding, though it is on the very edge of the cultivable area as one
approaches the Negeb; it is more difficult to envisage it also as a place
where Amos could have practised as a 'dresser of sycamore trees' (see
commentary on 7.14). It was of course a long way from the Northern
kingdom of Israel, where Amos's message was delivered, and there
have been some scholars who have argued that we should either envisage a different, northern, Tekoa (Koch 1982: 70), or regard the reference to Tekoa as a later editorial elaboration. The point is of some
importance for our understanding of the thrust of the book, for it has
often been argued that a major point of Amos's message, as against that
of, say, Hosea, was that he was a Southerner speaking in what will have
been to some extent an alien environment.

The next phrase, **which he saw…Joash of Israel** is usually regarded
as originating in a Deuteronomistic editorial process. It is striking that
Amos is said to have 'seen' his own words. Visions play an important
part in the book (cf. chs. 7–9), but the reference is probably more general than that. Strange though it may seem to us, it is likely that this was
a normal way of referring to words. In an analogous way, Isa. 1.1 refers
to the 'vision' of the prophet, when it seems most likely that the
reference is actually to the words that follow. Also somewhat ambiguous is the first reference to **Israel**. Later in the verse, when reference is
made to Jeroboam and Joash, it is clear that the Northern kingdom is
the referent. But the name 'Israel' came to be taken over by the Second

Temple religious community centred upon Jerusalem, and if that were the context of the gathering together of Amos's words that would be the natural meaning here.

Three kings are then mentioned: **Uzziah of Judah, Jeroboam son of Joash of Israel**. Modern scholars sometimes write as if ancient Israelites knew by heart the order and approximate periods of their kings, but this seems very improbable. Rather than a direct aid to the reader, this reference seems much more likely to be a deliberate allusion to what we know as 2 Kings. It is certainly possible that one reason for the lack of reference to prophets such as Amos in 2 Kings is that fuller details of their work were available in separate collections. On the other hand this is unlikely to be a direct reference to 2 Kings. The long-lived king of Judah there is usually named 'Azariah' (2 Kgs 15.1), though the name 'Uzziah' is also found (2 Kgs 15.32, 34), and this form is well-known from its use in Isa. 6.1. It could well be that recollection of the actual date of Amos's activity had been lost, and the editorial notes here and in ch. 7 can be seen as intended to indicate the appropriate period. Outside the editorial notes there are no indications of date.

Two years before the earthquake. Modern scientific skills have made it possible to work out when particularly severe earthquakes affected Palestine, and a date around 760 has often been proposed (Soggin 1987: 5-6). It has been argued that later references, apparently to the same earthquake (Zech. 14.5; Josephus, *Ant.* 9.222) show its severity. It may be so, but we should not exclude the possibility that these are intended as literary references rather than evidence for the effect of the earthquake. The latter part of Zechariah elsewhere shows links with Amos (cf. Zech. 13.5 with Amos 7.14), and Josephus is consciously dependent on what in his day was becoming 'Scripture'. In particular it would be unwise to treat the visionary picture in Zechariah of the division of the Mount of Olives as a neutral picture of the reshaping of the landscape. Even here in Amos caution is advisable. In 9.1 there is a reference to the shaking of the thresholds, and that has commonly been held to be a theological rather than a seismological phenomenon. The same explanation is certainly possible here.

If there was a particularly severe earthquake, it seems likely that the reference to it was a first attempt to see a 'fulfilment' of Amos's words, especially in such a passage as 9.5, which, whatever its original thrust, can readily be construed as referring to an earthquake. All the threats

inherent in the book were seen as being fulfilled in the devastation
brought about by an earthquake. Later, the Assyrian over-running of the
kingdom of Israel was seen as providing an even more dramatic
fulfilment of the threat of doom.

1.2. It would be possible to take the introductory **And he said** as no
more than a link to the first prophetic words in the book. It may well be,
however, that this phrase (one word in Hebrew) is intended as a conscious ascription to Amos of words already used at Joel 3.16 (MT 4.16).
The next expression,

> **The Lord roars from Zion**
> **and utters his voice from Jerusalem,**

in fact reads rather oddly in the context of Amos. Its other references to
Jerusalem are far from complimentary (6.1), and in any case Jerusalem
does not play a prominent part in the book. The origin of these words
with Amos has been defended (van der Woude 1982: 40, who notes the
similarity with 3.8), but it seems more probable that this should rather
be seen as part of the conscious redactional process bringing together
what eventually became the 'Book of the Twelve (Minor Prophets)'.
Amos was to be understood as proclaiming the same message as Joel.
Even if the immediate concern of his ministry was in the North rather
than in Jerusalem, the larger context of the two collections was the
same. The roots of this manner of referring to divine activity, and its
possible links with such Psalms as 46, have been explored more fully in
the commentary on Joel.

The thrust of the latter part of this verse has been very variously
understood. The usual sense of the verb *'abāl* is 'to mourn', and this
was the translation of RSV: 'the pastures of the shepherds mourn'. Some
such rendering seems desirable; NRSV **the pastures of the shepherds
wither** might simply be taken as reference to drought, whereas Murray
(1982: 208) has detected a 'larger picture' of desolation followed by the
triumph of Yahweh. In the passages he discusses the triumph is mostly
over foreign powers; in the doom-laden words of Amos we may see it
as a threat against his own people. One of the passages cited by Murray
is Isa. 33.9, and it is striking that there too we find reference to **Carmel**.
This makes it appear that such a reference had a place in the language
of the Jerusalem cult, and that that is its origin here rather than a simple
allusion to the plentiful forests of Mt Carmel. Jerusalem will prosper,
whereas Carmel **dries up**. These first two verses seem to form an intro-

duction to the book as a whole, probably from the standpoint of one or more Judaean editors; the main body of the book begins with 1.3.

1.3–2.16. This section clearly forms a unity. In addition to the commentaries the oracles directed against foreign nations were examined in detail by Barton (1980), and his work is still a most valuable resource for the better understanding of this section and the problems it raises.

An originally smaller block of material may have been extended by the introduction of additional nations to the original nucleus, and by elaboration of the oracle against Israel. Nevertheless it is not difficult to discern here a remarkably clear overall structure.

Each oracle begins with the 'messenger formula' (**Thus says the Lord**). It proceeds with the proclamation of judgment (**For three transgressions of** x, **and for four**). This mode of expression is clearly formulaic; we need not suppose that there was just that number of 'transgressions' in each case. The X/X+1 device has led some scholars (Wolff 1977: 95-98) to discern a wisdom background to the words of Amos, because the clearest examples of this usage are found in Proverbs (30.18 and elsewhere). The phrase which follows, *lō' 'ašîbennu*, NRSV **I will not revoke the punishment**, is of disputed meaning and will be considered more fully below. Within the overall outline it is clear that it is to be understood as part of the threat.

The most varied part of the denunciation is the next: the specific indictment, regularly introduced by the preposition *'al*, but then in the condemnation of each community combining remarkable variety with a number of recurring expressions. Yahweh's judgment is announced in terms of 'sending a fire', an expression slightly varied at 1.14, and missing in the denunciation of Israel. Details of the punishment vary, but a recurring motif is that of 'devouring' (*'ākal*) 'strongholds' (*'armonōt*). In most cases there is a concluding authentication: 'says the Lord (God)'. The omission of this phrase at the end of the oracles against Tyre, Edom and Judah has been one reason for seeing these as later additions, though in itself it is scarcely persuasive. A later redactor, wishing to imitate and develop earlier material, would surely not have neglected so obvious a feature of that material.

Before we look at the individual passages in greater detail, it is important to consider whether we should see in this material a new departure in Israelite prophecy or the adaptation of existing forms. When Barton wrote there was 'something like a consensus that here Amos is drawing on a tradition very old by his time' (1980: 8), but he

was able to show that none of the proposed contexts for such a tradition—holy war, ceremonies of lamentation, execration of enemies—
really stand up to close scrutiny. His own view was that while we cannot prove that this material in Amos had no predecessors, there was no
reason for supposing that it had, and he thought it unwise to attempt to
construct form-critical hypotheses to account for the form of the material (Barton 1980: 15). In this present commentary, where we are more
concerned with the shape of the book than with attempts to trace the
experience of the individual Amos, it may suffice for us to note that
there are no close and obvious links with other material, biblical or non-
biblical, save for the fact that other prophetic collections also contain
oracles against foreign nations. But whereas several such collections
show close links with one another (within Jer. 46–51, for example,
there are verbal and thematic links with both Isaiah and Obadiah) this
material in Amos has very few such links (though cf. the commentary
on vv. 13-15 below). In general it is quite distinctive and can
legitimately be treated in its own terms.

Various attempts have been made to see a particular literary structure
in the order of the oracles. Paul (1971) detected in the section extending
from 1.3 to 2.3 'a concatenous literary pattern' and claimed to detect
particular 'agglutinous elements' which produced a specific pattern,
with key phrases linking specific oracles together. Such a judgment is
inevitably subjective; it is impossible to lay down objective criteria for
deciding that linkages of this kind are intentional, though some of his
suggestions will be noted below. An analogous, though strikingly different, set of proposals for the 'rhetorical analysis' of this material has
been put forward by Meynet (1998: esp. 256-308). Though ingenious,
the use of classical rhetorical models does not seem to lead to any striking exegetical insights. It is perhaps also worth noting that such detailed
literary analyses seem to be very distant from the traditional picture of
Amos the simple shepherd.

One particular understanding of these oracles should be mentioned,
though it will not be pursued in detail. It has been suggested that for the
proper understanding of this material we should have in mind the
Davidic–Solomonic Empire, and the obligations laid by the Israelite
kings on their neighbours. These obligations, which can broadly be
described as 'covenantal', were not being honoured by the neighbouring states, and this is the background against which Amos's denunciations should be understood. Such a view, put forward in its most

detailed form by Polley (1989), makes a more confident judgment of what can be known of the Davidic period than many modern scholars would accept, and seems unlikely in terms of straightforward historical reconstruction. Whether it in any way influenced the final editors of our book, who will no doubt have been aware of the traditions embodied in the books of Samuel and Kings, must remain open to speculation.

One other repeated feature of these oracles requires attention, not least because of the dispute it has caused. It is the repeated phrase *lo 'ašibennu*, This has been much discussed. Barton (1980: 17-18), following Wolff, lists six different understandings of 'this highly elliptical phrase' which have been proposed. Since it features in all the oracles, including that against Israel, a very specific meaning is unlikely. The problem is not a matter of establishing the meaning of rare vocabulary, for the verb *šub* is one of the commonest of Hebrew verbs. The expression is probably formulaic in some sense. NRSV, **I will not revoke the punishment**, follows a long tradition in different English translations, and is approved by Barton, though in the end he favours 'I will not rescind my decree', arguing that this envisages a decree of destruction upon the nations listed, which could not now be rescinded.

1.3-5. The first oracle is directed against **Damascus**. The nature of the relation between Israel and the Aramaean kingdom of which Damascus was the capital is ambiguous. This is indeed one of the reasons why the historical picture presented in the books of Kings has come to be questioned. There Damascus is pictured as a long-standing enemy of Israel. But according to the best-known Assyrian records from the ninth and eighth century BCE they are to be understood as allies. Both the Kurkh Stele and the Black Obelisk of Shalmaneser III (858–824 BCE) mention Damascus and Israel as among those who joined to oppose his attacks on Syria–Palestine. While it is not difficult to envisage states which were often at enmity joining together in the face of a greater external threat, we are at least reminded of the very partial nature of our knowledge of this period and its history. It may well be that the editors of our material wished to emphasize the uniqueness of Israel, which could not be pictured in alliance with pagan nations.

This then raises the more general question whether the references in our verses are to specific historical events, or are more broadly pictured as the kind of behaviour of which human beings were only too capable. Various attempts have been made to discover particular events underlying these charges. Thus, Barton (1980: 26) identifies 'three main periods of Aramaean expansion' which are worthy of consideration if we wish to make a specific identification. Two of these seem too remote from any plausible background for Amos (either the individual or his collected oracles) to be worthy of detailed scrutiny. The first is the attempt to trace the origins of the Aramaean activity referred to here back to the time of Israel's united monarchy and the early years of the divided kingdoms. Thus Clements (1975: 65) had this in mind when he spoke of events that had 'taken place long before the time of Amos, probably more than a century before'.

Barton's second period is the mid-ninth century BCE, associated particularly with the reign of Ahab. At first sight this seems a plausible link, for the story in 1 Kings 22 apparently has Ahab and the (unnamed) 'king of Aram' each claiming possession of Ramoth-gilead, which ties in well with the reference to **Gilead** here. But closer scrutiny greatly weakens this proposed link. For a start it is at odds with the Assyrian references mentioned above, which have Ahab and the Aramaeans as allies in the ninth century BCE. Further, most recent studies of 1 Kings 22 have raised considerable doubts as to whether its link with Ahab is original; the ruler is normally described as 'the king of Israel', and is only named as 'Ahab' at v. 20. This might be a dramatic device, revealing the name of the previously anonymous king, but seems more likely to be part of the later editorial process linking this story into the larger collection of material relating to Ahab. Barton's conclusion (1980: 27) is that 'we cannot say with certainty that Ahab did not fight the Aramaeans, but the difficulties in supposing him to have done so are very considerable'.

It seems likely, then, that if we are to seek a historical background to the condemnation of the Aramaeans, it must be at a slightly later period, for which the evidence is 'copious but confused' (Barton 1980: 31). We need not here go into the details of this 'copious' evidence, for we should remember that the only specific accusation is that the Aramaeans **have threshed Gilead with threshing sledges of iron**.

Whatever the background of 1 Kings 22, it clearly emerges from that story that Gilead was a disputed area between Damascus and Israel, an area in which wars will have been fought and, no doubt, atrocities committed. It is striking that the verb *duš*, 'to thresh', comparatively rare in its metaphorical use, is also found in the sense of 'exterminate' in another description of the Aramaeans' behaviour (2 Kgs 13.7). There is no question of direct literary dependence in either direction, but it does seem as if a common motif was in use here.

The use of **threshing sledges of iron** may also owe more to literary vision than to the details of agricultural practice. Such sledges were normally wooden (*IDB*, IV, 636); the introduction of 'iron' implies atrocities committed against the population. It is a nice irony that what is here presented as an atrocity will be envisaged in much more positive terms when Israel itself is pictured as waging war in this way (Isa. 41.15).

The wrongdoing is very briefly described; the divine response is spelt out much more fully. **Hazael** and **Ben-hadad** were both known as kings of the Aramaean kingdom; the episode referred to in 2 Kgs 8.7-15 describes a coup by Hazael against Benhadad, and there has been much speculation how many rulers of each name can be traced. It seems quite inappropriate to use the present allusion to try to reconstruct particular historical circumstances. Either these were well-known ways of referring to these foreign rulers, or Amos can be seen here, as elsewhere, as a kind of drawing out of the significance of some of the events described in 2 Kings.

In v. 5 the threat seems to become more specific, but once again we note that certain stereotyped verbs are used: **send, devour, break, cut off**. It is possible, though difficult to prove, that a word-play with covenantal language can be traced. The standard terminology for covenant-making was *kārat bᵉrīt*, literally 'cut a covenant'. Here we have *bᵉriah* ('**gate bars**') and the idea of 'cutting off' (the same verb, *kārat*). This suggestion would be more persuasive if covenant language were an established feature of Amos. *yōšeb* is conventionally translated as **inhabitants**, the plural in English being acceptable, understanding the Hebrew singular in a collective sense. But the parallel with **the one who holds the sceptre** in the following line suggests that the meaning may be 'ruler'. (Gottwald 1980: 513 listed this passage and v. 8 among several places where he considered this to be the most likely translation.)

The remainder of v.5 has divided interpreters. Some have seen it as a basis for reconstructing the history of the middle years of the eighth century, with **Beth-eden** in particular being identified as an area, Bit-Adini, which was disputed between Israel and the Aramaeans. Similarly, the reference to an **exile to Kir** has been linked with various Assyrian threats.

Though such reconstructions are not impossible, they invite a measure of scepticism. They seem to imply the figure of Amos engrossed in the ancient equivalent of broadsheet newspapers or television, and seeing in the news of the day a fulfilment of his understanding of the divine purpose. The renderings offered by Wolff (1979: 129), 'Sin Valley' and 'House of Pleasure', seem to catch the sense better. Possibly these were known Aramaean features, and no specific contemporary historical reference can be gained from them. Once again we note a possible link with 2 Kings, where 19.12 has 'the people of Eden' among those who suffered deportation. More specific is the link with 2 Kgs 16.9, describing the king of Assyria carrying the people of Damascus 'captive to Kir'. In Amos this takes on the quality of poetic justice, for Kir is said to have been the place of origin of the Aramaeans (9.7). They are pictured as sent back whence they came. We do not know where Kir was, and it may well be that the author of Amos was similarly ignorant. The point being made is a literary and theological rather than a geographical one. The theme of exile, or enforced deportation, is one that runs through the whole book.

1.6-8. Just as Damascus, its capital, had stood for the whole Aramaean kingdom in the previous oracle, so here **Gaza** symbolizes the Philistines. If we accept the widely held view that the Philistines were organized as a pentapolis, a league of five cities, we note that, of the other members of that coalition, **Ashdod**, **Ashkelon** and **Ekron** are mentioned in the oracle. The omission of Gath might imply that it was no longer an active member of the coalition, or had lost its independence (Wolff 1979: 158). The first part of v. 6 is identical with v. 3 except for the changed place-name, and this repetition is to be expected in a series of oracles such as this. More surprising is the fact that the remainder of the verse shows very close links with v. 9, and it is commonly held that one or other must be secondary. The question naturally arises whether such repetition is in fact to be understood as implying secondary additions, or whether it should rather be seen as a deliberate literary device, but since the usual source-critical view is that it is v. 9 which is more likely to be an addition, we may postpone discussion of that problem for the moment.

The theme of **exile** is a common one in the Hebrew Bible, and it is natural to find bitterness against those who engineered such deportations. The adjective *šalemah*, found both here and in v. 9, seems to imply a complete deportation (NRSV, **entire communities**), but we have no means of knowing whether some specific atrocity was in mind, or who the communities so delivered were: was it the captives in a particular war, or the inhabitants of some unfortunate spot? The logistics of a deportation from Philistia, West of Judah, to **Edom**, South-east of Judah, has led to the proposal to read 'Aram' instead of Edom, but this scarcely engages with the deeper problem of whether or not we should look for specific historical events behind the poetic oracle.

On similar grounds it would probably be unwise to attempt to identify these communities; the focus of attention was on the perpetrators of the act rather than those who were its victims, who might have been anyone with the misfortune to be captured.

Verse 7 is substantially identical with v. 4, the difference emerging from the fact that the names of individual Philistine rulers did not enter into the tradition underlying the Hebrew Bible in the same way as Hazael and Ben-hadad had done. This pattern of basic similarity with slight differences is also found in v. 8, including the likely sense of 'ruler' for *yōšeb*, **inhabitants**. The announcement that even **the remnant of the Philistines shall perish** is language characteristic of oracles of this kind, emphasizing the completeness of the punishment, and should not be taken as a clue to particular historical developments. Indeed, in more general terms it seems right to see these similarities as evidence of a conscious literary style.

1.9-10. The oracle against **Tyre** is the first of those widely regarded by historical critics as a secondary addition, and it is certainly the case that it displays features which differentiate it from other material in this section. Thus in historical terms it is not easy to envisage any circumstances at the time of the conventional dating of Amos that might have given rise to such an oracle. Whereas references to Damascus and the Philistines as enemies of Judah and Israel are readily found in the books of Samuel and Kings, such material is lacking for Tyre. There is no reference to dealings with Tyre in the books of Kings after the time of Solomon, whose cession of 'twenty cities' to Hiram of Tyre caused friction between the two rulers (1 Kgs 9.11-13), and that scarcely seems relevant here.

Obviously it is possible that historical events otherwise unrecorded are alluded to in this oracle, but we should also note the literary reasons which have led critics to question the originality of this section. Three such reasons are commonly alleged (Barton 1980: 22, following Wolff): the way in which the *'al*-clause (**because...**) is expanded in this

and the also-suspect Edom oracle with finite verbs; the very generalized
character of the threat of punishment in v. 10, quite lacking the specifi-
city of, for example, vv. 7-8; and the absence of the concluding formula, **says the Lord (God)**. In addition v. 9 seems substantially to
repeat what has already been said against the Philistines in v. 6, and the
expression **remember the covenant** in v. 9 is found frequently in
writings held on other grounds to be late (especially the P strand of the
Pentateuch, e.g., Gen. 9.15-16), but not in those from the time of Amos.

Various responses to this understanding are possible. (Auld 1986: 43
comments helpfully on some of the views expressed by those who
accept the historical-critical approach, but who nevertheless maintain
the originality of all the oracles against foreign nations.) Clearly the
stylistic variants and the omission of the final phrase are of limited
significance; sometimes these points are seized upon as if they demonstrated the existence of a particularly crass later editor/redactor who
failed to notice some of the basic features of the text being edited. We
may note that, even among those oracles almost universally accepted as
part of the nucleus, the form of the final phrase varies; usually 'says the
Lord', it is extended at v. 8 by the addition of the word 'God'.

This raises the more general question of repetition, which must surely
have an important part to play in any poetic collection, and is certainly
not a criterion for the rejection of a particular passage. Indeed various
attempts have been made to use such repetition as a cue for detecting
particular literary patterns in the collection as a whole (Paul 1971, elaborated further in his 1991 commentary, though he joins many other
scholars in treating the Judah oracle, 2.4-5, on a different basis).

One further comment is necessary. Our discussion thus far has
assumed virtually without argument the validity of the historical-critical
assumption that a primary concern of the commentator must be to probe
the pre-history of the text rather than the form in which it has come
down to us in the Hebrew Bible or in later translations. Characteristically, critical commentators have emphasized those points that made it
seem likely that this oracle against Tyre, together with those against
Edom and Judah, are secondary, unlikely to be from Amos himself. In a
remarkably similar way, commentators of a more conservative disposi-
tion have claimed that Amos could indeed have uttered these oracles.

But perhaps our concern should be a different one. We have already
seen some reasons for doubting how much we can know of Amos as an
individual and of his precise historical setting. What has come down to

us is a book, or perhaps more accurately a chapter of a larger book, the Book of the Twelve. From as far back as we are able to trace, the oracles that have been questioned have been an integral part of Amos—there is no textual evidence that suggests their omission—just as Amos has always been regarded as part of the Book of the Twelve. Whether we regard the text we are concerned with as 'canonical', that is, as having special authority for certain faith communities, or primarily as a piece of ancient literature, the form in which we have it has always included these oracles, and our reflection upon this text should regard them as an integral part of it.

Little further comment is needed upon the content of the oracle. As in v. 6 we have the difficulty raised by 'delivering communities to Edom'. If we were to take this literally the logistical problems would appear to be insuperable, and this no doubt underlies the proposal in BHS to emend to 'to Aram'. A better approach may be to see lying behind both v. 6 and this verse the conviction, widespread in the Hebrew Bible, of Edom as the characteristic centre of betrayal (cf. Obadiah, the next element in the 'Book of the Twelve', as well as passages like Ps. 137.7). The theme will be taken up again in the last section of the book (9.11-12). To be delivered to Edom was in itself a punishment. It is no surprise that in its final form the collection of oracles also includes words directed against Edom.

1.11-12. As we have noted already, on a historical-critical analysis there are features of this oracle against **Edom** that have caused it to be regarded as secondary. However that may be, we should certainly expect, on both historical and literary grounds, that a collection of oracles against the surrounding nations would include words directed against Edom. Historically, the relation between Israel and Edom seems often to have been a tense and bitter one, while in literary terms the references to Edom at the end of Joel (3.19 [MT 4.19]) and throughout Obadiah make it natural for us to expect such reference in the intervening book of Amos also.

Though the type of wrong alleged against Edom is similar to that found in the earlier oracles, after the formulaic introduction the actual language used is different. **He pursued his brother with the sword** is so general that it is impossible to know what is envisaged; we note only the tradition that recurs in the Hebrew Bible from Genesis onward of Jacob (Israel) and Esau (Edom) as brothers.

Though its general sense is clear, the following expression *wᵉšiḥat raḥamayw* is more difficult to render confidently. The verb *š-ḥ-t* usually has the sense of 'spoil' or 'ruin'; a sense such as 'stifle' or 'deaden' is possible here, though NRSV **cast off** seems rather free. It is noteworthy that REB offers a very different rendering of the whole section: 'sword in hand and stifling their natural affections, they hunted down their kinsmen'. Andersen and Freedman (1989: 266-67) accept the normal meaning of the verb, but offer 'his allies' as a possible meaning of its object. On their own admission there are no biblical examples of this usage, though it is found in postbiblical Hebrew and has been proposed by several scholars. Some such meaning is undoubtedly required, but whether this is the appropriate way in which to arrive at it must remain doubtful.

The difficulty here arises partly because the next phrase is also disputed, as is already noted by the margin of NRSV. As is stated there the normal meaning of the verb *wayyitrop*, would be 'and his anger tore'. Older commentators such as Cripps pointed out that it would be more accurate to read the Hebrew as meaning 'he tore his anger', and that 'without doubt the text should be emended' (Cripps 1955: 131). His emendation, to *yittor*, is close to that proposed by BHS: *wayyittor*. More recently, however, the tendency has been to retain MT. Barthélemy (1992: 642-43) discusses the phrase at length and he and his colleagues, in the curious voting system they have adopted to uphold or question the reliability of the MT, have given the received text three 'a' votes and three 'b', suggesting a high degree of confidence. In particular they support the understanding proposed by Wolff, taking 'anger' as the subject and offering the reading 'his anger plunders continuously'. This enables them also to account for the curious feminine form in the next line, making it a verb dependent on the feminine noun *'ebrāh*, 'his wrath is ever alert'. Certainty on these textual points may never be reached, but the general sense is clear enough, of the implacable hatred displayed by the Edomites.

This leads naturally enough into the prophet's announcement of Yahweh's corresponding punishment. **Teman** and **Bozrah** are best understood as surrogates for the land of Edom as a whole; Teman provides an obvious link within the Book of the Twelve with Obadiah 9, where different but comparable punishment is announced. The reference to Teman at Hab. 3.3 seems to be of a very different kind, since it is there proclaimed that 'God came from Teman'. Should we read this as implying that God's presence with Israel implies his departure from

Teman? Bozrah is probably not found elsewhere in the Book of the Twelve; the reference in AV to 'the sheep of Bozrah' (Mic. 2.12) is taken by the great majority of modern translations, e.g. NRSV, REB, to mean 'sheep in a fold (*'ozrāh*). Punishment of Bozrah is, however, threatened as part of the condemnation of Edom in Jeremiah 49 (see esp. vv. 13 and 22). All of this implies that this passage should be seen as part of a larger pattern of condemnation of Edom, rather than as a reference to some specific event.

1.13-15. The condemnation of **the Ammonites** follows the by now familiar form. The name of this Transjordanian people is preserved in the capital of the modern state of Jordan, here mentioned as **Rabbah**. They are always described in the Hebrew Bible as *b^{e}nē 'ammon*, literally 'sons of Ammon'. Hebrew apparently did not have a gentilic to refer to the nation as a whole, though it is doubtful whether this different form implies any inherent difference of perception. They were separated from Israel by the great Rift Valley, the *biq'ah*; it may be fanciful to see an allusion to this when they are condemned because they **ripped open** (*biq'am*) **pregnant women**. The description of Nahash the Ammonite king in 1 Sam. 11.2 suggests that the Ammonites were traditionally regarded as liable to commit atrocities. It is certainly striking that here and in other parts of the oracles against the nations (e.g. 2.1) the whole community is condemned for offences that must have been committed by individuals. It is in any case not clear how such an act would enable any nation to **enlarge their territory**. It seems likely that this was a standard form of condemnation applied to one's enemies (cf. 2 Kgs 15.16, where the same war crime is mentioned). Apart from any possible wordplay it may well be that the reference to the atrocity is a vivid way of describing the ruthless waging of war.

The pattern of the preceding oracles is maintained with the threat of **fire**. There are not many close links between the foreign nations material in Amos and that found elsewhere in the Hebrew Bible, but we noted in the preceding oracle some similarities with Jeremiah 49, and these are found again here, in connection with Jer. 49.1-6, a passage 'concerning the Ammonites'. The suggestion has indeed been made that this link has affected the text at this point. Wolff (1979: 131) proposed reading *w^{e}šilaḥti* ('I will send'), as in the other oracles, e.g. 1.12, maintaining that MT *hitṣattī* is taken over from Jer. 49.2, but this seems too wooden: minor variants of this kind are common enough in Hebrew poetry.

Shouting on the day of battle may not convey the intended impression; the *tᵉrū'ah* is not just a noise, but a formal war-cry; here Wolff's 'fanfare' does bring out the sense. Later on in Amos the theme of the 'day of the Lord' will become prominent; we cannot be certain whether an allusion to it is intended here, because we are uncertain how far in popular understanding it involved warfare such as is described here. In v. 15 it would be unwise to suppose that a particular deportation of an Ammonite **king** and **his officials** is being described. Exile was a recurring threat to the leaders of a state defeated in war.

This assumes, of course, that the Masoretic pointing is correct in seeing here a reference to the Ammonite king. The consonantal text *m-l-k-m* could be pointed as 'Milcom', and a reference seen to the Ammonite god of that name. Some Greek manuscripts understood the Hebrew in that sense, even adding a reference to the priests of that God (Wolff 1979: 131-32), and, if this reading were to be supported, it would add another example to the list of allusions in Amos to the books of Kings; here cf. 1 Kgs 11.5.

2.1-3. The last of the oracles against foreign nations relates to **Moab**, Judah's neighbour East of the Dead Sea. After the usual formulaic introduction we encounter what appears to be the most specific of all the accusations levelled against the nations in these oracles. **He burned to lime the bones of the king of Edom**. The identity of the 'he' is not specified; this is to be envisaged as a national crime. As so often with the references in these oracles, two main lines of interpretation present themselves.

One possibility is that there had been a war between Edom and Moab, of which we otherwise know nothing, and which had culminated in the atrocity here described. There is nothing inherently implausible about such a view; the problem is not only our ignorance of any possibly relevant events, but also it assumes that Amos's audience would both be able to pick up the allusion and be directly concerned with such atrocities.

Perhaps then the other line of interpretation is more plausible: that we should see here, as in a number of other references in this opening section, an allusion to the books of Kings. Here the obvious reference would be to the events described in 2 Kgs 3.27, though there it is the king of Moab's own son who suffers the fate described. Bartlett (1973: 254) obviates this difficulty by proposing a re-pointing of the Hebrew text. Where MT has *melek 'ᵉdōm*, we might read *mōlek 'ādām*, implying a human sacrifice. This is ingenious, but lacking in any direct support-ing evidence. In any case the passage does reflect the respect for human remains which is characteristic of the Hebrew Bible. The killing of an enemy is only to be expected, but his remains should be treated with respect. Not only that: if we retain MT it is very striking that the atrocity committed against Edom should merit condemnation. One might have supposed, in view of the harsh attacks on Edom that we have noted, that this act would be regarded as a just reprisal. Instead, it is strongly con-demned.

The form of punishment is the same as in the preceding oracles. Here a specific place-name, **Kerioth**, is provided. It is given the definite article both here and in its other usage at Jer. 48.24, 41, and some have supposed that the reference is more general—'their towns', as in NEB following LXX. But Kerioth is referred to also in the Mesha stele, so it is likely to be the right sense here. (It is restored in REB.) It may well have been a sanctuary of the Moabite god Chemosh. Its site is unknown. As in 1.14 the picture is given of a military onslaught upon Moab.

2.4-5. The secondary nature of the oracle against **Judah** has been widely recognized in critical scholarship, even by those commentators inclined to accept the genuineness of all the material directed against 'foreign' nations. We should notice straightaway that the present pas-sage exists in all forms of the book of Amos that have been handed down to us; in canonical terms, that is to say, this is an integral part of Amos. On the other hand, for those whose concern is to explore the likely development of the book to its final form, and still more for those who are concerned with an individual Amos living in the eighth century BCE, then this passage can be regarded as a secondary addition. The plurality of different possible readings should be recognized and respected.

The reasons for the suspicion that has attached to these verses are not far to seek. In the most general terms we may note that it was part of the developing perception of the prophetic ministry that prophets should have warned their own people about the dangers of **rejecting the law of the Lord**. In later interpretation the deportation to Babylon came to be seen as an 'exile', interpreted as a punishment brought on God's people by their failures in obedience, despite prophetic warnings. Since the book of Amos presumably reached its final form in a Judahite setting, whatever its earlier history, it was regarded as inevitable that

some such words should have been uttered. This picture of the exile and
its causes is frequently described as 'Deuteronomistic', since it corresponds very closely with the picture offered to us in the books of Kings.
Such a linkage is suggested by the use of the relatively rare verb *tā'āh*,
in the causative (hiphil) form, both here (**they have been led astray**),
and in 2 Kgs 21.9 (NRSV, 'Manasseh misled them'); Manasseh was, of
course, regarded in the books of Kings as bearing a very great responsibility for the evils that befell Judah. Characteristic also of the viewpoint
of Joshua–2 Kings is the concern expressed here, of the present generation following **the same lies after which their ancestors walked**. The
'lies' may refer to the attraction of gods regarded as false, or may simply be a more general form of condemnation. These links with the
'Deuteronomistic history' seem clear. We should be aware that
'Deuteronomistic' is a slippery term, which takes on a variety of meanings in different contexts (Coggins 1995: esp. 141-43), but provided
that that danger is recognized it can serve to designate a particular theological viewpoint.

Turning more specifically to our passage, we note that there are no
references here to war crimes of the kind that have featured in all the
preceding oracles. Where they have concentrated on offences against
neighbouring states, here the offences are against God. Basic is the
rejection of the *tōrāh*. Opinions differ sharply on how precisely we are
to understand this 'torah'. Eventually, of course, the term was used to
stand for the central part of the Hebrew Bible, our 'Pentateuch'. It is
scarcely likely that that will have reached its final form by the time of
this oracle, but it is not impossible that the term was already being used
for the nucleus of such a collection early in the Second Temple period.
This might be suggested by the parallel with *ḥuqqayw*, **his statutes**,
which might seem to point to a body of ordinances. But of course torah
was already a word in widespread use, to denote 'guidance' in more
general terms. (One must be careful of giving too much weight to ety-
mologies, but it is worth noting that the word comes from a verb *yarah*,
one of whose basic meanings is to give guidance by pointing the
finger.)

The oracle ends with the announcement of judgment, here in its
shortest form, as in 1.10, 12.

2.6-8. As is very well known the series of oracles ends with a condemnation directed against **Israel**, usually taken to imply the Northern
kingdom during the time of the divided monarchy. Perhaps this was its

original thrust, though at some point it surely came to be applied to the whole community of religious believers who took on the name of 'Israel' (Wolff 1979: 164-65). There is no clear evidence how soon this title came to be applied to the religious and social group centred upon Jerusalem.

Many modern commentators have allowed their imagination free rein as they have described the way in which the pleasure that greeted Amos's oracles against foreign nations turned to indignation when they heard themselves being condemned. Such eloquence will not be attempted here; we know too little about an individual character called Amos, or his relation to these oracles, to make such a pursuit profitable. Whether the readers (or, perhaps more probably, hearers) of these words expressed comparable frissons is also difficult to decide; not much is known about the impact of dramatic writing upon its hearers in the ancient world. What we can say is that this device of treating the writer's own nation as being on a par with other, commonly-rejected, neighbours is an unusual one, in both the ancient and the modern worlds, and its effect remains striking. This is still true, even though, or perhaps because, the charges against Israel in the remainder of this chapter seem on the whole to be less serious than those directed against the foreign nations. It is often maintained that what is referred to are essentially social offences, though that is not always clear (cf. in particular the commentary on 2.7-8). But certainly, in comparison with what has preceded, they are what might be described as 'small-scale' offences, though the punishment threatened is apparently greater.

The opening words of the oracle against Israel follow the standard formula, but the similarity with the earlier material breaks down when the reasons for **punishment** are spelt out, and the links are never restored. There is nothing to correspond with the 'sending of fire' that has concluded all the previous passages. There is a real sense in which the passage we are now looking at introduces us to the concerns of the rest of the book. The rhetorical question at 9.7, 'Are you not like the Ethiopians to me, O people of Israel?' in effect brings the central part of the book to an end, and the implied answer, that Israel is indeed like the Ethiopians, is also the point of the structure of the oracles against the nations.

When we come to examine the charges in detail, greater problems arise. It is clear that acts of injustice are involved in selling **the righteous for silver, and the needy for a pair of sandals**, but the first difficulty comes in deciding the identity of the victims. NRSV 'righteous' is the natural rendering of *ṣaddīq*, but it then raises the question: would it have been acceptable if those enslaved had not been righteous? In other words, are we dealing here simply with an abuse of judicial process, or are more specifically 'religious' issues involved? NEB resolved the difficulty in one way by translating *ṣaddīq* as 'innocent'. This took the whole context as being judicial, and provided a helpful means of entry to the social concerns that were regarded as the main theme of Amos. Justice must be available to rich and poor alike; innocence rather than earthly power was the basis of one's standing before God. REB has modified the translation to 'honest folk', retaining the general sense, though now in a less specifically juridical context. It certainly seems to fit well with v. 7a, where **poor** and **afflicted** are treated as victims.

The implication of such a reading as this is to see this part of the book, along with 8.4-6 in particular, as essentially a protest against various economic developments which were bearing down heavily on some parts of society. During the Iron Age there was an increasing tendency toward centralization of the economy, and the demands of 'higher authority' will often have placed heavy burdens on those used to a more local economy, based on subsistence and mutual self-help. If such were the underlying thrust of this passage it would be possible to depict Amos either as an economic Luddite, if one held that progress to a market-based economy was necessary and desirable, or as a staunch upholder of traditional values, if one took a different view.

This may not, however, be the whole of the story. Whereas the semantic field of *'ebyon* normally embodies a reference to material lack, there are indications that it might have a more specifically religious reference. Apart from two passages in Amos, here and 5.12, a similar usage may be detected in Ps. 37.14, where the poor are linked with 'those who walk uprightly', and more generally in the usage in the Dead Sea Scrolls, where it is becoming a self-description of the faithful community (DCH 1.104 offers several references). It has been characteristic of religious groups in their devotional language to describe themselves as the poor, and it may be that we see an early stage of such a designation here in Amos.

The other pairing in v. 6 is also unexpected. **Silver** can be understood as denoting something valuable, but may also suggest the judicial context noted as one possibility for *ṣaddīq/'ebyon*. To **sell...for silver** may

well imply bribery of the supposedly impartial judge. That in itself may
indeed be plausible, but it then fits awkwardly with **a pair of sandals**,
which has usually been understood as the barest necessity of a poor
person. A common understanding is that what is envisaged is debt-
slavery, the condemnation being based either on the injustice of depriv-
ing the poor of their basic needs, or on using the mechanism of debt-
slavery for so trivial a matter. Reference is often made to the 'Book of
the Covenant' in Exodus 21–23, but there is no direct reference there
which throws light on our passage.

Verse 7 is printed as poetry by NRSV and most recent translations,
but BHS considers it overloaded and prints it as prose, with suggestions
of elaboration of a possible poetic original. Perhaps more serious is the
difficulty in making sense of the Hebrew as it has come down to us.
NEB footnote justifiably has 'Hebrew obscure'. The phrase here used is
found again at 8.4, and the translations offered by NRSV are closely
similar. Here we have **trample the head of the poor into the dust of
the earth**, which certainly sounds like an appalling atrocity, and might
be a metaphor for generally oppressive behaviour, but it is not easy to
see its relation to the Hebrew.

The problem is with the verb. MT has *šo'ᵃpīm 'al-'apar-'ereṣ*, which is
translated by AV 'that pant after the dust of the earth'. The verb, a participial form, is understood to be *š-'-p*, the normal meaning of which is
'to gasp, or pant', and BDB 983b took this rendering to be 'hyperbole
for extreme avarice'. It was already widely supposed that there was a
by-form of this verb, with the meaning 'crush, trample upon', but BDB
noted that it was 'strangely' applied to this verse, and recourse was had
to the versions to obtain a more acceptable sense. As so often the
difficulty with this solution is that it is likely that the ancient versions
were themselves trying to resolve a text that did not make obvious
sense. One resolution of the difficulty, supported tentatively by BHS, is
to modify the text to find a form emanating from the verb *šūp*, 'to
bruise or crush', and this might be supported by the main LXX reading
ta patounta, 'who trample'. This of course brings us back to NRSV,
which has achieved its version by inverting the order of the next two
phrases in Hebrew. 'The head of the poor' is preceded by the preposition *bᵉ*, 'with' or 'in', but that is regarded as a likely addition by BHS
and ignored by NRSV (and its parent translations). Many other proposals have been made (Barthélemy 1992: 681-84 offers an extended
discussion of the textual history of this passage and 8.4), but certainty is

impossible. The best we can say is that some form of oppression, probably by perversion of the course of justice, is implied.

In the first half of v. 7 the general sense is clear, the text much less
so. In its second half the situation is reversed. The text is regarded as a
possible addition by BHS, but it is clearly part of the present form of
the book, and there is no dispute about its make-up. We can say that it
is part of a condemnation, but exactly what is being condemned is far
from clear. Translated literally we should have, 'and a man and his
father go to the girl'. That is to say, NRSV , **father and son go in to the
same girl**, has introduced three changes into the text. The order of the
generations is reversed; the introduction of 'in' makes a much more
specifically sexual allusion; and the word 'same' is introduced. (REB,
we may notice, is even more imaginative: 'Father and son resort to the
temple girls'.)

Let us consider these modifications in turn. First, it is undoubtedly
more usual to mention a father before his son, but this should surely
alert us to the unusual order of the Hebrew. Might it be that the theme
here is of the son in some way dishonouring his father? In a culture
such as that of ancient Israel, where categories of honour and shame
were of great importance, this point should certainly be kept in mind.
Secondly, some caution is required in the face of the almost universal
assumption of translations and commentators that the offence being
condemned is explicitly sexual. The Hebrew here is simply 'go to', and
nowhere else in the Hebrew Bible is this phrase used with unambiguous
sexual connotations. That the girl is in some sense a victim we need not
doubt, but we may reserve judgment whether the offence is primarily
sexual, whether it be the rape of an unwilling partner or some form of
prostitution. Finally, as we have seen, nothing in the Hebrew corresponds to the word 'same' in English, still less is there any indication
that the girl in question is one of 'the temple girls', as REB so deli-
cately expresses it. It has been argued with regard to Hosea that we can
see traces there of a practice wherein women engaged in sexual inter-
course with strangers prior to marriage as a means of bringing new life
to the community (Wolff 1974: 14-15), but that is quite different from
anything here. *na'⁺rāh* is a young woman. The noun carries no implication of irregular sexual practice; if that were implied we should have
expected some such word as *zonah*. There is thus no reason for associating such a term with the practice of temple prostitution, despite the
claim of Soggin 1987: 48, that 'the [definite] article with "woman" also

indicates that this is a current term for sacred prostitute'. She would have been of marriageable age, but not yet married.

We should be wise to admit our uncertainty as to the exact nature of what is here being condemned, and in particular as to why two generations are being singled out. It is possible that the offence is sexual, but if that is so it is more likely that the concern is with the exploitation of the woman rather than with the sexual act in itself. (The Hebrew Bible is much more relaxed about a variety of sexual partnerships than some modern readers would wish it to be.) More probably, if the condemnation is taken with what precedes, the young woman is to be seen as a victim of oppression; it might have been impossible for her to achieve a respectable marriage if she were not a virgin, and she is, like those referred to earlier in the verse, a defenceless victim.

We should also bear in mind the possibility that we should take this condemnation with what follows rather than with what precedes, in which case some wrong religious practice may be involved. Perhaps 'the girl' is a slighting way of referring to someone venerated as a goddess (Meynet 1998: 258). This would tie in with the assertion that the behaviour described means that **my holy name is profaned**. If we take the view that the main thrust of Amos's polemics is religious (thus particularly Barstad 1984) then it would be natural to see in this the misuse of the holy place. Admittedly this would provide an additional argument in favour of a temple context for the previous condemnation. But a more general reading is also perfectly likely. It was not only in a formally religious context that God's holy name might be profaned; every kind of oppressive action had the same consequence.

This same ambiguity between specifically religious and more 'social' offences continues in v. 8. Thus, one reading would want to stress the social injustice implicit in the retention of **garments taken in pledge**. According to Exod. 22.26-27 (MT 22.25-26) a cloak taken in pawn should be returned before nightfall, 'for it may be your neighbour's only clothing to use as cover'. In an analogous way, the **fines... imposed** would be the product of a corrupt system of justice, and those responsible for such wrongdoing would here be condemned. This may indeed be a legitimate reading of the verse, though it would be unwise to bolster it by deleting the phrases **beside every altar** and **in the house of their God** as is proposed by BHS.

Wolff (1979: 134) also sees these phrases, together with 'so that my holy name is profaned' in v. 7, as later additions, perhaps offering us a

clue to the formation of the Book of the Twelve, when the clearly cultic
concerns of Hosea shaped the reading of the later elements in that book.
But it is also possible to read this verse in its present form so as to show
that the cultic reference is primary: the basic ground for condemnation
is not so much the social injustice as the fact that these wrong-doings
are occurring in places devoted to the worship of God. (It is noteworthy
that even today, in places where formal religious observance is often
minimal or non-existent, a vague but widespread feeling persists that
some otherwise acceptable actions are not appropriate in a church
building.)

Some commentators (e.g. Mays 1969: 47) have laid stress on the
reference to *'their* God', and seen in this a link with condemnations of
Canaanite worship. This seems to read a good deal more into the text
than it will bear. There are few references in Amos which could be
interpreted as condemnations of Canaan and its religious practices, in
the way that Hosea has often been read, and in any case it is far from
clear that any distinction can legitimately be made between Israelites
and Canaanites as two potentially opposed groups occupying the same
territory when this material was shaped.

It will not be possible within the limits of this commentary to give
detailed consideration to 'reader-response' questions, but the section we
have just looked at certainly leads to such issues. To take just two
examples: first, there can be no doubt that much of the modern interest
in Amos arises from the fact that this text has been discerned as a great
cry on behalf of those who are oppressed. Naturally enough, those who
are themselves oppressed, together with those who take seriously the
many social evils in the world, will seize on this section as a biblical
vindication of the rightness of their cause. They will have a natural dis-
position to read these verses in that sense rather than as concerned with
what they see as obscure religious wrongs. Secondly, women may well
seize on the male-centred attack in v. 7. Though the men are condemned, it is from a male viewpoint, and no concern is shown for the
woman who is the victim. 'The girl got lost in the theological accusation' (Sanderson 1992: 208).

2.9-11. The difference from the earlier oracles, aimed against foreign
nations, now becomes very marked. This section stresses the uniqueness of Yahweh's relation to this, his own, people. Rhetorically the
point is made by the shift from third- to second-person reference. There
is some manuscript support for reading *mipp^{e}nēkem*, 'before you', in

the first line of the verse, though MT *mipp^{e}nēhem*, **before them,** is followed by NRSV and most moderns. But by the beginning of v. 10 the
shift to direct address is clear: **I brought <u>you</u>.** The hearers or readers of
this oracle can no longer suppose that its reference is to someone else, a
long way off and a long time ago. The specific illustration of this is
provided by the theme of God's saving acts in the people's history.
Several links with the picture offered in the Deuteronomistic History
have already emerged, and here this is taken further.

There has been much discussion of the historical **Amorites,** but here,
as in Deut. 1.7 and 2 Kgs 21.11, the overall picture is clearly of Israel
as a nation which had entered the land from outside, and of the
Amorites as the existing inhabitants. Those existing inhabitants were
frequently envisaged as being of gigantic stature and phenomenal
strength, and though this picture is not elsewhere specifically applied to
the Amorites, it is a standard trope in accounts of this kind to exagger-
ate the power of the defeated enemy. The link may have been made by
way of Sihon and Og, the 'kings of the Amorites'; Og in particular was
one of the 'Rephaim' and had an 'iron bed' of exceptional size (Deut.
3.11). All such opposition had been swept aside.

The possession of **the land of the Amorite** is now set in the context
with which we are most familiar: as the climax of the deliverance **out
of the land of Egypt** and the period of **forty years in the wilderness.**
Elsewhere the time spent in the wilderness is regarded as a punishment;
here it is set out as an example of God's leading his people, a necessary
preliminary to giving them the promised land.

Characteristic of Deuteronomy and the Deuteronomistic History also
is the veneration for **prophets**; here, as in Deut. 18.15, they were **raised
up** by God, and came to be regarded as the messengers by whom God
warned the people of the dangers of turning away from him (2 Kgs
17.13, and many other passages). Whether the figure of Amos himself
was recalled in the book as a prophet is an issue we shall have to consider at ch. 7. The reference to **nazirites** is more unexpected. The
arrangements for nazirite vows are described in detail in Numbers 6,
but in the Deuteronomistic History the only person described as a
nazirite is Samson (Judg. 13.5; 16.17). Samuel has often been considered as a nazirite in modern discussions, but the biblical text nowhere
describes him as such. It is possible that an allusion to Samson is intended here, for the people are charged in v. 12 with making the nazirites
drink wine, and Samson is certainly not pictured as an abstainer. But

there are no obvious cross-references, and it seems best to see this reference as a distinctive contribution of the Amos tradition. In Amos itself prophets will feature again, but there is no further reference to nazirites after v. 12.

The somewhat cryptic phrase, **Is it not indeed so, O people of Israel?**, with which v. 11 ends is perhaps best understood as an appeal that the people should acknowledge the truth of the charge brought against them. Whether there is also an implicit call for repentance is more difficult to decide; such calls, though not unknown, are hardly a characteristic feature of the prophetic collections.

2.12. This verse is printed as poetry by BHS, but it looks like a prose reflection upon the failure of the people to respond to the divine initiatives. Any example that might have been set by **the nazirites** is made nugatory if they are made to **drink wine**; the prophetic office becomes void if they are prevented from speaking. Elsewhere the picture we are offered is that the prophets could not be prevented from speaking; Elijah in his encounters with king Ahab comes to mind. But the point being made here is clearly a rhetorical one.

2.13-16. Now comes the announcement of judgment, introduced by the characteristic *hinneh*, the 'behold' of older translations, beside which NRSV **So** seems rather feeble. The certainty of the judgment is also stressed by the form with the personal pronoun *'anoki* spelt out: **I will certainly act**. This dramatic effect is slightly weakened for us by the fact that we cannot be quite certain of the nature of God's action, for the verb used, √*'ūq*, is found only in its two occurrences in this verse. NRSV, **press down/presses down** is noted in the margin to be of uncertain meaning. Already classified as 'dub.' by BDB 734a, many suggestions have been made in more recent lexicons and commentaries either for emending the text, or for discovering the meaning of the word. Thus Holladay (1971: 268) gave 'be hindered' or 'totter' as the main proposals, while noting a recent suggestion 'be bogged down'. Soggin (1987: 49) provides a useful summary of the suggestions made by earlier commentators as to this 'well-known *crux*'. He concludes that it is likely that there is a reference to the earthquake mentioned in 1.1, and proposes the translations, 'tremble' or 'split'. In the context of the whole book this is probably the most attractive reading; if we wish to differentiate between a nucleus of poetry and later prose editorial expansions this becomes less satisfactory, since references to the earthquake are largely confined to the prose material. For want of a more convincing explanation, however, it will be followed here.

Whatever the solution of the linguistic problem, the overall picture it introduces is clear enough. Total disaster is announced. All the abilities seen as signs of human achievements will be brought to nothing. Here the emphasis is on male achievements; the fate of women is spelt out later (4.1-3), but in any case it is noteworthy that it is those of some social distinction who are addressed. All who are listed here: **the swift, the strong, the mighty, those who handle the bow, those who ride horses** and **those who are stout of heart**—all these would have been regarded as being **among the mighty**. They were the successes of society. Whether the opposition to them reflected a different social background on the part of the poet, or whether we should see in Amos himself a 'dissident intellectual' (Blenkinsopp 1996: 79), set against the customs of his fellows, it is clear that the divine verdict against Israel is pictured in very harsh terms. It seems quite pointless to try to spell out some specific set of historical events which were in mind here.

There is not a great deal in the detail of this verdict which need detain us. Verses 14-15 emphasize the inadequacy of human strength, and a climax is reached in v. 16, where even the bravest of fighting-men will be reduced to panic. As is often the case with biblical references to nakedness it is not clear whether or not this is to be taken literally; most probably it here means that fighting men have had to jettison weapons and equipment, without which they feel **naked** in the sense of being exposed to any threat. The whole picture is one of the natural order being turned upside down, and it will be important to have this in mind when we come to consider how the three psalm-like poetic fragments (4.13; 5.8-9; 9.5-6) function within the overall theme of the book.

3.1-2. A new section clearly begins here, though the overarching theme of judgment against Israel will run through virtually the whole of the book. The introductory formula **Hear this word** is one which will recur on several occasions, and may well have been among the guidelines used in the mediaeval division of the book into chapters (cf. 4.1; 5.1), though 3.13 also has an introductory 'Hear'. The prose of the first verse serves to spell out more precisely those against whom Yahweh's indictment is addressed. It is another warning against any supposition that this book was aimed against the Northern Kingdom only; the **people of Israel** is very specifically identified as **the whole family that I brought up out of the land of Egypt**. If we read this in conjunction with the Deuteronomistic History, as several indications have already shown to be appropriate, it is clear that all the 'tribes' were involved. The Exodus from Egypt had been the formative event in shaping the community, and much of their subsequent religious history seems to have been spent in hearing words **against** them.

The poetic couplet which follows needs to be read in conjunction with 9.7, which at first sight might seem directly to contradict this verse. That is probably too neat a conclusion; apart from the dangers of reading poetry as if it conveyed precise information, much turns on the sense given to **known** here. It is obvious that it does not imply God's ignorance of other nations; it is a relational word. Some have seen it as expressing the notion of covenant, but this theme is not characteristic of Amos, and it is better simply to recognize in this verse the assertion of a relation. That relation has been jeopardized by the Israelites' behaviour to such an extent that by the end of the book the Israelites are no more closely related to their God than are the distant Ethiopians.

Families of the earth is a curious phrase. *mišpaḥot* is an unexpected word for what is apparently a reference to other nations, for its usage is largely confined to particular social groupings within Israel. Again, *'adamah* is not the word we should expect to find if the reference is to all the world: most commonly it refers to a group within Israel. However, this phrase is found twice in Genesis (12.3; 28.14), with reference to the blessing conveyed via Abraham and Jacob, and one could almost read our passage as a revocation of the privileges promised to those ancestors. In any case the **therefore** is important as spelling out a basic concern of much of the Prophets, that privileges involve responsibilities.

3.3-8. A series of questions runs through this section, described by Wolff (1979: 183) as a 'didactic disputation'. The form is no longer that of the classic prophetic oracle, with the prophet speaking as the messenger from God. Rather it seems as if we are being invited to overhear a discussion between a teacher and students: not exactly a Socratic disputation, but analogous in its intention. The main block of the section is a series of rhetorical questions, each inviting the answer 'No', and leading the hearers/respondents into a position where they are forced by their own logic to recognize the divine origin of the events they see around them. The editorial hand is most apparent at v. 7, which at one level might seem to contradict what has gone before, since here the direct divine causation implied by the rest of the passage is replaced by the assertion that all God's **secret** actions are actually revealed **to his**

servants the prophets. But it is also possible to make sense of the passage as it stands, as we shall see when we have considered the development of the preceding questions. In any case we may note at the outset that the thrust and elegance of this passage have always been recognized as a powerful argument against the traditional picture of 'Amos the simple shepherd' as its author. The command of rhetorical technique is on any showing impressive.

Verse 3 is clear as to its general point, that for **two** (presumably unrelated) people to **walk together** will not be a matter of chance. This is the effect, for which a cause must be acknowledged. As a translation NRSV, **they have made an appointment** seems to be too reminiscent of the doctor's surgery, but is probably the right understanding of the verb *yāʿad*. Many scholars have proposed an emendation to some form of the verb *yādaʿ*, 'know', to provide a link with Yahweh's 'knowing' in the previous verse, so that we should have a sense such as 'Do two walk together without knowing one another?' (Soggin 1987: 57). But it seems better to retain MT which is well supported by the versions.

The cause-and-effect theme is very clear in v. 4. All English versions have to use some form of the word **lion** in each half of the verse, but two quite different words are found in the Hebrew: *'aryeh* and *kᵉpîr*. When lions were sufficiently common in Palestine to be a realistic threat to daily life, the language differentiated between different forms of the species. The most obvious sign of a lion was its **roar**, and that is described here with the same word (*šāʾag*) as was used of Yahweh himself in 1.2. This may offer an interesting sidelight on one perception of their God. It is alleged (e.g. by BHS) that *mimmᵉʿonōtō* (**from its den**) is an addition, presumably because the regular metre is disturbed. But more recently greater caution has prevailed about amendments based solely on metrical grounds, and we may simply note that the word makes good sense in its context and is clearly part of the text handed down to us.

There are stronger grounds for textual emendation in v. 5, where the word *paḥ*, **snare**, is found in each half of the verse. Direct repetition of this kind is rather unusual, and the first occurrence seems not to be found in some LXX manuscripts, so it could be that the first line is better translated 'Does a bird fall to the earth...' On the other hand we shall notice that direct repetition is also found in v. 6 (*bᵉʿir*, **in a city**), so that stylistic generalizations could be misplaced.

Regrettable though we may find it, bird-snaring was a fact of life in ancient Israel. With v. 6, however, we move to situations where divine intervention, denoting some crisis, would more immediately be recognized. The questions also are differently formed, though the basic theme of cause-and-effect remains. The passive form of 6a suggests that *any* threat to a city is being considered, but 6b is much more specific: no **disaster** can **befall a city** without divine responsibility. The section beginning at v. 3 might at first have seemed to be a digression; now it has been shown to be nothing of the sort. By implication, all the apparent coincidences and 'ordinary' events alluded to in the series of questions are held to be part of the divine plan. Sometimes the nature of that plan is self-evident; at other times it needs to be interpreted by chosen intermediaries.

It is in this context that it is possible to see v. 7 as fitting into the overall structure of the section. It appears to be in prose and may indeed be the work of a later glossator, as the great majority of commentators has held. But whereas very often to assign a passage to a glossator has been to give it a much diminished status, frequently with scathing remarks about the incompetence of the glossator, here the overarching cause-and-effect concern of the passage is developed in a particular way. God's action is indeed claimed as the basic cause of events, but it is not arbitrary. People would be able to detect it much more readily if only they paid attention to **his servants the prophets**. This phrase is very characteristic of the Deuteronomistic history. Once again 2 Kings 17 appears as a chapter that can profitably be read in conjunction with Amos; 2 Kgs 17.13. is here especially relevant. In particular the prophets gain their insight by being privy to the divine *sod*, translated here as **secret**, but the sense is perhaps better brought out by REB 'plan', or by NRSV itself at Jer. 23.18, 22, 'council'. The underlying idea of God working out his plan in company with reliable counsellors is one found in much of the Hebrew Bible. Later those counsellors will be described as 'angels'; here the 'prophets' are the appropriate support group.

The section ends with an inclusio, the **lion** that **roared** in v. 3 being linked with the theme of prophecy. Once again it seems as if very strong claims are being made for the prophetic role; the last word, *yinnabe'*, seems to imply more than simply 'be a prophet' or 'act out the prophetic role'. We have been told that the prophets have access to the divine secret, and so to **prophesy** is to proclaim God's word for each situation.

3.9-11. Here we come to one of the earliest traceable developments in the history of interpretation of Amos. NRSV follows MT in translating **Proclaim to the strongholds in Ashdod**, and is surely right to do so. The 'strongholds' provide a link back to the foreign nations material in ch. 1, and 'Ashdod' was referred to at 1.8. It seems proper to expect that a reference to a foreign neighbour will once again lead into a condemnation of Israel. It is noteworthy, however, that RSV here had 'Proclaim to the strongholds in *Assyria*', basing itself upon the Greek, and a number of popular modern translations have followed the same course. MT is surely to be followed as the appropriate text, but the reference to Assyria is a striking one. If the poems which make up our book of Amos were being attributed to an individual who lived in the mid eighth century BCE, as for example is done in 1.1, then it was natural to suppose that when the Assyrian threat followed a generation later it must have been foreseen by him. He was, after all, a prophet, and we have just been assured that 'God does nothing without revealing his secret to his servants the prophets'. The insertion of a reference to Assyria was an obvious way in which to follow out that logic. We might regard it as an early example of reader-response criticism.

In fact, of course, the primary thrust of this passage is not a concern with threats from foreign nations, but an invitation to foreign nations to observe the evils rampant in Israelite society. The 'mountains of' **Samaria** are to be the place of assembly from which they can **see** these evils. NRSV follows BHS and the Greek text in emending 'mountains' to 'Mount', but that fails to recognize that this is theological geography: the idea of gathering on encircling heights to see the fate of those below. The phrase is found again at Jer. 31.5; again the geography is theological, though the context is very different.

The general sense of the last part of v. 9 is clear, but its detailed make-up less so. The normal meaning of *m^ehumāh* is 'panic', so that its plural form found here is unusual; NRSV **tumults** probably catches the sense, of the general confusion brought about by Yahweh's action against his own people. The natural sense of *'ašūqim* would be 'oppressed' but BDB 799b listed this as one of three passages (cf. Job 35.9; Eccl. 4.1) where the form appears to be an abstract plural, and so gives us NRSV **oppressions**.

The charge against the community follows in v. 10. In the phrase **know how to do right** the last word (*n^ekōḥāh*) has the sense of what is straight, and so the charge here is probably of dishonesty. The Israelites

too have **strongholds**, and the reference here supplies a link not only
back to v. 9 but also to the 'strongholds' of ch. 1. Now it is taken further; the strongholds are not simply metonyms referring to the place;
here they have become storehouses for the ill-gotten gains of **robbery
and violence**.

The reference to **strongholds** provides yet another link, this time
with the following announcement of judgment. This is the first occurrence in the book of the **therefore** (*lākēn*) which introduces a statement
of inevitable punishment. It will recur several times in later chapters.
Here the Hebrew text is less clear than NRSV **an adversary shall surround the land** might imply. In an extended discussion of this verse
Barthélemy refers to 'la leçon ramassée et difficile de M' ('the
condensed and difficult reading of the MT') (1992: 648-49). MT *us^ebīb*,
if correct, would be the only example in the Hebrew Bible of the
preposition *sābīb*, 'round about' being used in the singular construct
form and NRSV's emendation to the related verbal form is widely
supported. But we then have the uncertainty of knowing what or who is
to 'surround the land'. LXX read 'Tyre', and this may be an example of
another early stage in the history of interpretation, from a time
(unknown to us) when Tyre posed a particular threat to Israel. More
difficult to decide is whether the reference of the Hebrew is to a specific
'adversary', in which case the Assyrians would naturally have come to
mind, or, perhaps better, to 'adversity'.

The remainder of v. 11 is also not without its textual difficulties. A
widely followed emendation (BHS) is to read the verb as passive (*hūrid*
instead of MT *hōrid*), providing a better parallel with the last line: 'your
strength shall be brought down'.

3.12. This verse is printed as prose by NRSV, but at least the first part
seems to be in a balanced rhythmic form. Its underlying assumption is
that a **shepherd**, who was hired and given the responsibility of looking
after flocks, had to produce evidence if any of his charges had been
mauled by predators. Exodus 22.9-12 sets out the kind of situation
envisaged, and it is possible that our passage reflects knowledge of
Exodus. It is also possible that what is alluded to here may have been
well-known practice, for which no specific reference need be cited.
Nevertheless, in view of the wealth of intertextual references that we
have already noted in Amos this link with Exodus should certainly be
borne in mind. In any case we notice again the reference to a **lion**; the
word used here (*'ari*) is a variant on that found in vv. 4, 8 (*'aryeh*),

where the allusion to Yahweh himself was unmistakeable. Here surely we are also meant to see that the predator being alluded to was not just any wild animal; Yahweh himself was envisaged as devouring his people. On the other hand we need to bear in mind that the Hebrew text has the usual word for 'shepherd', *ro'eh*, at this point rather than the *noqed* of 1.1. NRSV, like other English versions, has 'shepherd(s)' on each occasion. It is not clear if there is any specific reason for the particular bits of the animal that were rescued. The meaning of *b^edal* is uncertain, as the noun form occurs only here, but the context makes NRSV **piece** a fairly certain rendering.

Problems arise with the last part of the verse. There is dispute as to how the verse should be divided; it is also textually difficult, and is indeed described by Soggin (1987: 61) as a 'classical *crux interpretum*'. NRSV prints the verse as a continuous whole, but BHS wishes to divide it, ending the first section with 'so shall the Israelites be rescued', and taking 'those who dwell in Samaria' as the beginning of a separate section. This has the advantage of avoiding the curious phrase **the people of Israel who live in Samaria**, and removing the problem of what it should mean to be rescued **with the corner of a couch and part of a bed**.

But the problem is, of course, only removed, not solved. We might suppose that the general picture being set out is that those now comfortable will be reduced to more marginal conditions, but that seems rather feeble when compared with the usual vividness of this poetry. It may be tiresome to be forced to the *pe'āh*, or 'edge' of the bed, but it is scarcely to be compared with the fate of the unfortunate sheep in the first part of the verse.

Part of our difficulty here is uncertainty in knowing whether the reference here is to the people's experience before or after their punishment. Andersen and Freedman in their translation (1989: xxx) suppose that a parallel is envisaged between the two halves of the verse, so that the mauled pieces of sheep are to be likened to the fate of the Israelites:

> only the corner of a bed
> only the *dmsq* of a couch.

But the uncertainty of this rendering is already apparent from their failure to translate *dmsq*, and in their commentary they admit that the 'remainder of the verse is beyond recovery' (1989: 408). it has even been suggested that *d^emešeq* in its MT form reflects mediaeval usage— what was customary at the time of the Masoretes. No attempt will be

made here to claim to resolve the various interrelated problems; we
may simply note, if it is any consolation, that the recognition of
difficulty goes back at least as far as the ancient Greek translators, for
LXX transliterated the last word in the Hebrew text, *'āreś*, whose normal
meaning is 'couch', as *hiereis*, 'priests'.

3.13-15. The textual difficulties of vv. 11-12 lead to some uncertainty
as to the proper division of the next section. One possibility is to take
v. 13 as the conclusion to what has preceded, with the juridical language (**testify**) relating to the charges implicit in the preceding verses.
If that were so, then the solemn formula at the end of this verse, **says
the Lord God, the God of hosts**, regarded by BHS as an addition,
could be taken as integral to the text and rounding off the oracle. In this
understanding the *ki* with which v. 14 begins (not translated in NRSV)
would be seen as asseverative, 'Surely **on that day**'.

An alternative possibility, implied by NRSV, is to take vv. 13-15 as a
unit. In any case v. 14 offers the first example of another link between
Amos and the books of Kings: polemic against **Bethel**. Those who have
attempted to explore the redactional history of the material (e.g. Coote
1981; this is his 'Stage B') have proposed that one particular layer of
material can be identified as opposed to Bethel, but this kind of reasoning is bound to be speculative. What we can say is that both in Amos
(cf. also 4.4; 5.4-5; 7.10-13) and in Kings (notably 1 Kgs 12–13; 2 Kgs
17.28, and the account of Josiah's 'reform' in 2 Kgs 23) bitter hostility
against Bethel is expressed. There was clearly rivalry between the
shrines of Jerusalem and Bethel, and it is interesting to recall that the
claim of Bethel to ancestral approval (Gen. 28.11-22) was not (?could
not be) expunged from the tradition. What other reasons there may have
been for such a tension we do not know.

The present threat is that the **horns of the altar** would be **cut off**.
These were the protuberances found at the corners of altars, to which
fugitives could cling in the hope of sanctuary, as did Adonijah, who
'went to grasp the horns of the altar', seeking sanctuary against Solomon's revenge (1 Kgs 1.50). In effect the pronouncement is that Bethel
would offer no sanctuary, for there would be no altar and no cult place.

This brings us to one of the tensions in Amos, between a primarily
religious and a primarily social frame of reference, that we have noted
before. Whereas v. 14 is concerned with the cult at Bethel, v. 15
appears to be aimed at the luxuries enjoyed by the ruling classes.
Though it is possible that reference to both **winter house** and **summer**

house implies a condemnation of the rich who can afford to have different houses suited to the different seasons, it is perhaps more likely that what we have here is a merismus, using opposite extremes to bring out the idea of totality: 'all houses' will be torn down in the devastation that is threatened. At the same time an element of intertextualtiy should not be excluded with each name. First, the only other place in the Hebrew Bible which mentions a 'winter house' (*bet haḥōrep*) is Jer. 36.22, which provides the context for king Jehoiakim destroying Jeremiah's scroll of words from the Lord, and it is natural enough to read each of these texts with the other in mind. Then, secondly, the word *qayiṣ*, 'summer', is the word that will provide the basis of the wordplay in 8.1-2, with the judgment that 'the end [*qeṣ*] has come'.

The last part of the verse also provides links with the condemnations found in the books of Kings. The exploitation of **ivory** is in modern times condemned on ecological grounds; in ancient Israel it seems to have functioned as a particular symbol of luxury. The reference to Solomon's 'great ivory throne' at 1 Kgs 10.18 comes just at the point at which that king's commendable lavishness where the temple was concerned is turning to condemnable extravagance where his own lifestyle was involved. If the reference to Solomon is ambiguous the reference to Ahab and his 'ivory house' (the singular of the phrase used here) (1 Kgs 22.39) is certainly one of condemnation.

Less clear is the following phrase, *battim rabbīm*, which would normally mean 'many houses' (so NRSV margin) A widely supported emendation (cf. BHS) is to *hobᵉnīm*, 'ebony'. This word is found only at Ezek. 27.15. The strength of the suggestion lies in the fact that in the Ezekiel passage 'ivory' is found in the parallel colon; its weakness is the lack of any positive support, either in the versions or elsewhere.

4.1-3. One of the best known passages in Amos follows. Before we look at its contents we note that it is another of the extended passages introduced by **Hear this word** (cf. 3.1; 5.1). (3.13 offered a partial parallel, but there the introduction was simply 'Hear'.)

The next phrase has become well known, not least because it has almost universally been regarded as very androcentric, with a view of women that should be regarded as offensive. This may indeed be so, but before approaching the text in that way we should notice first a very different kind of understanding of this section that has been proposed. Barstad notes that just as in 5.2 'maiden Israel' is a way of referring to the whole community, so here we should think of '*all* inhabitants of the northern capital, rather than some separate group among them' (Barstad 1984: 40, italics in original). This is part of his larger hypothesis of much of Amos being concerned with the condemnation of Canaanite cult practices. Though it gives a different angle on some disputed passages, it also raises fresh difficulties, as we shall see later in this verse. Barstad's interpretations of individual passages deserve more attention than they have commonly received, but it still seems doubtful to what extent a mainly cultic reading of Amos is appropriate.

If, then, we take this passage as it has been traditionally understood, as addressed to the upper-class women of Israelite society, what precise nuance should we detect? **Cows of Bashan** sounds thoroughly offensive, and was perhaps intended to be so. First of all, though, we should bear in mind that whereas in modern English to call a woman 'a cow' ought to be completely unacceptable, a man might be rather flattered by being called 'a bull'. His prowess, whether sexual or athletic, might thereby be praised. Similarly, in the Hebrew Bible it is widely thought that one designation for God, 'Mighty One of Jacob', for example at Gen. 49.24, was a reference to his bull-like character. Animal metaphors were often used when describing human beings, and were by no means necessarily negative (Sanderson 1992: 208). Again the description of them as 'of Bashan' invites comparison with the expression 'bulls of Bashan'. In Ps. 22.12 (MT 22.13) the Psalmist's enemies are so described, but this is simply a way of conveying their strength and power. So in our passage 'cows of Bashan' may be an at least partly admiring reference to the well-formed bodies of the women. Slimness was not regarded as a desirable characteristic, as far as we can judge, either by women themselves or by the men who no doubt sought to shape their self-perception.

The charge against these women places them in **Samaria**, not Bashan itself, which was, of course, east of the Jordan. This provides a link with 3.9, 12, which is taken further when we find the same verb '*āšaq*, **oppress**, being used. Thus far, the point seems to be that the poet wishes to emphasize that the women among the higher strata of society are as guilty as their men-folk, and will receive comparable punishment.

It is the last line of the verse that seems to have aroused the indignation of commentators. Vivid pictures have depicted these women lolling in comfort and demanding that their husbands, wearied by their own efforts in oppressing the poor, should satisfy their wife's needs first of all. It is an inherently improbable picture, both from what we know of Israelite society, and from the very modest base of the two words in the Hebrew text, 'Bring that we may drink'. If we were to suppose that a rough English equivalent might be 'Come on, let's have a drink', we should retain the condemnation of those who oppressed those less fortunate than themselves without the implication that the women were in some way deserving of additional condemnation.

In any case their fate is not an enviable one. One of the strengths of Barstad's cultic understanding is that in each of the texts concerning women the **holiness** of the Lord is in some way impugned (cf. 2.7). Here, however, the traditional understanding as implying God's very nature seems acceptable.

The details of the remainder of vv. 2-3 are obscure but their general import is clear enough: the women are to suffer some degrading and painful punishment. The *sinnot* may be either 'shields' or **hooks**, and the next phrase, NRSV **the last of you**, could bear almost any of the meanings associated with the word 'behind' in English—one's posterity, the sense of 'every last one of you' implying totality, a remnant, or, more personally, the anus. If the last is the primary sense the use of **fishhooks** will have been painful indeed.

Presumably the **breaches in the wall** imply that their city has been invaded and destroyed. Through the ruins they are forced out, either 'one after another' or **straight ahead**, in the way that a line of captives is prevented from straying out of the path laid down. **Harmon** is presumably a place-name, but no site of this name is known, and many proposals for its identification have been put forward of places all over the Near East, 'clear evidence of the ingenuity of the commentators' (Hammershaimb 1970: 67). Alternatively it may be a common noun meaning 'dunghill' (so NEB/REB). *DCH* 2.593 offers various emendations which would achieve this sense.

4.4-5. Irony is a dangerous figure of speech to employ in a religious context, for there will usually be some hearers who take one's subtleties literally, but irony is surely intended here. **Come to Bethel** may well have been the summons to worship at festival time. Here we are once again confronted with the anti-Bethel polemic noted at 3.14. With it, here and again at 5.5, is linked **Gilgal**. It is commonly held that there may have been several sanctuaries with this name, since its meaning, 'a circle (of stones)' could well have had sacral associations. More important than concern to identify the place is the recognition that, as with

Bethel, what is taking place is a deconstruction of other traditions
within the Hebrew Bible. Just as Bethel had links with the patriarchs, it
was at Gilgal that the newly-arrived community had been circumcised
and 'the disgrace of Egypt' rolled away (Josh. 5.9). Claims on behalf of
the Jerusalem sanctuary in the form of polemic against any potential
rivals might go to considerable lengths. Whatever their past traditions,
now even to go to such places is to **transgress**, indeed, to **multiply
transgressions**.

Four ironic ritual requirements follow. At least, we assume that they
were ironic. One possible reading is to suppose that what is condemned
here is excess of zeal. Whereas the norm was that festivals might be
celebrated on great occasions, characteristically three times a year
according to the cultic calendars in the Pentateuch, here either the people themselves are eager to turn up much more frequently, or perhaps
those in control of the sanctuaries are urging them to do so.

But the charge in v. 5 seems to have been modified. Now it appears
that the accusation is that the worshippers are failing to observe the
requirements of the Torah. Leviticus 2.11 is the most specific of
numerous texts that warn against bringing an offering made with
leaven. To the charge of excessive zeal is now added one of wrong ritual practice. The unexpected nature of this juxtaposition has led some
scholars to understand the preposition (*me-*) in the word *meḥāmeṣ* as
having a partitive sense, 'without', and this is followed by REB, 'Burn
your thankoffering without leaven'. This is ingenious, but it then
becomes very difficult to see what it is that the worshippers are doing
wrong. The usual reading should be retained. If one is attacking rivals
they can be held to be guilty of a great variety of wrongs without consistency being required.

4.6-11. Here we have a series of short oracles in which to an even
greater extent than previously the poet claims divine authority. He can
speak with total confidence in God's name. The passages are linked by
the way in which each of them ends with the identical refrain, **yet you
did not return to me, says the Lord**. The English translation is appropriate in itself, but has the unfortunate effect of obscuring the link with
the refrain in 1.3 and each of the oracles against foreign nations, NRSV
'I will not revoke the punishment', though NB the margin, which draws
attention to the fact that the Hebrew is 'cause it to return'. The link with
the earlier passages is surely a deliberate one. The semantic field of the
verb *šub* is not easy to identify, but it seems that the people's failure to

'return' is one cause of God's not holding back their inevitable punishment. The verb is used again in a dramatically different sense at 9.14
(see the commentary there).

In the first of the oracles the ironic element continues. *niq^{e}yon*,
cleanness, normally has positive connotations, but here a very unwelcome cleanness is promised: cleanness of teeth because there is **lack of
bread** to make them dirty. *ḥoser*, 'lack', is found in the curses of Deut.
28.48, 57, also in a context of threatened famine. **All your places** may
simply be a way of saying 'everywhere', or may denote more
specifically cult-centres.

Verses 7-8 develop the warnings of famine. God's gift of **rain** is
often taken as a sign of blessing in the Hebrew Bible (e.g. Lev. 26.4).
Here it is **withheld**, a clear indication of divine disfavour. Whereas in
v. 1 to have 'something to drink' was taken for granted, now there is
nothing. It is striking that whereas Hosea, especially ch. 2, went to great
lengths to stress that it was Yahweh rather than any rival deity to whom
the blessings of fertility were due, here the poet finds no difficulty in
speaking in Yahweh's name as raingiver. The latter part of v. 7 and 8a
(from **I would send** to **not satisfied**) are set out by BHS as prose and
thought likely to be an addition. This may be so, and it is certainly the
case that this oracle is more extended that those which follow in 9-11.
Nevertheless we notice the x/x+1 numerical device (**two or three**) used
also in chs. 1–2.

Verse 9 has a picture of crop failure, a natural sequel to the drought
of vv. 6-8. Again it is taken for granted that Yahweh controls the suc-
cess or failure of the crops. **Blight and mildew** seem regularly to be
associated with one another (cf. Deut. 28.22). NRSV follows the majority of commentators in emending the next word, *har^{e}bot*, into a verb,
laid waste, presumably *heherabti* or the like, for its normal sense
'multitude of', makes no sense here. The ingenuity of Barthélemy in
retaining an acceptable sense for the MT has been stretched here, but he
suggests that the first verb (**I struck you**) governs this part of the sentence, and that we should translate 'the multitude of your gardens', a
phrase intended to show the extent of the devastation (Barthélemy
1992: 656-57). **Fig trees and olive trees** were a regular symbol of agricultural prosperity; we are reminded of the Rabshakeh's promises to the
beleaguered people of Jerusalem in 2 Kgs 18.31-32. But they will be
devoured in the same way as God had sent a plague of **locusts** on the
Egyptians in Exodus. The locusts provide a further link with Joel (here

gazam is the 'cutting locust' of Joel 1.4).

The theme of **pestilence after the manner of Egypt** implied by the locusts, is taken up more specifically in v. 10. The two Hebrew words *deber bᵉderek* illustrate well changing fashions in the study of the Hebrew Bible. Older commentators maintained that the similarity of the two words was evidence of an error in transmission, so that, for example, BHS suggested either that the second word should be deleted entirely or at least emended to *kᵉderek*. More recently, however, the tendency is to suppose that the soundplay here is deliberate and should not be modified.

As to the remainder of the verse as far as the refrain, the general sense is clear but the detail rather obscure. As is noted in the NRSV footnote there is a reference to 'the captivity of your horses'. Both this and the following reference to **the stench of your camp** presumably refer to some military defeat, but we have no means of being more precise.

The section ends with a reference to the destruction of **Sodom and Gomorrah**, the famous cities whose overthrow, described in Genesis 19, became paradigmatic for events pictured as the carrying out of divine destruction. References to the cities are usually in southern traditions (e.g. Isa. 13.19), but as we are here primarily concerned with the final form of Amos, which certainly passed through southern editorial hands, that need not be a problem. The verb *hapak*, **overthrew**, is regularly used of the destruction of Sodom and Gomorrah, as the prime example of God's overthrowing of enemies. It is an accurate translation, though it reads curiously in English, to have both the first person **I**, and also a reference to what **God** had done, as if God were not perceived to be the speaker. But the text should be preserved, against the attempts of BHS to tidy it up.

Amos has not given rise to many characteristic Enlgish expressions, but the phrase 'a brand snatched from the burning' originates here, though AV had 'plucked out' for 'snatched'.

4.12. The function, if not strictly the form, of what has preceded, is as a series of curses. Now their implementation is announced. BHS regards the whole of the latter part of the verse as a probable addition, but this seems quite unacceptable; the tension is piled up in the first part by the repetition of **I will do**, and this is followed by the summons to **prepare to meet your God**. This warning, much favoured by devisers of modern wayside religious posters, has been given a covenantal sense by some scholars (Brueggemann 1965: 13-14). It would thus be seen as an assertion that the covenant is now abrogated and Israel's special status set aside. This conveys the general sense well enough, but we need to be cautious about a specifically covenantal reading in view of the lack of *bᵉrit* language in Amos. We have noted a number of points at which there are close similarities in outlook between Amos and the Deuteronomistic History. We need to bear in mind also that there are important differences, and the lack of direct reference to the people's covenant status is one such.

4.13. This verse has obvious links with two later doxological passages (5.8-9; 9.5-6); less clear is the reason for its being placed in its present context. It is probably right to see that after the harsh judgments of the preceding verses the poet thought it appropriate here to include a 'hymnic affirmation of divine justice'. This expression was used by Crenshaw as the title of his study of the three doxologies (Crenshaw 1975). The God in whose name the poet has been speaking is here claimed to be the universal creator, so that such judgments as the withholding of rain (4.7) and the plagues described in 4.9-10 are wholly within his power. This is the kind of God whom Israel must expect to meet.

This verse, therefore, makes good sense in its immediate context, but it is also important to see its links with the other doxologies. In each passage the use of relative clauses in English translation (**the one who**...) renders participial constructions in Hebrew, and this is characteristic of hymns in the Hebrew Bible. The passages are also linked by the expression **the Lord is his name**, found in slightly variant form in each of them. Characteristically, this common feature has been interpreted by scholars in radically opposed ways; some have seen it as evidence that the three passages once formed part of a single hymn, whereas others have taken this as pointing to the later binding together of originally separate poems by the addition of a common refrain. Certainty in this matter is impossible to reach; all that we can say is that together the doxologies play an important part in Amos, emphasizing that behind the danger that God might be a destroyer lay a basic belief in his achievement as a creator.

This is brought out immediately by the use of the verb *bara'*, **creates**. As is well known, this verb is found only in the context of divine activity, most characteristically in Genesis 1 and other parts of Genesis conventionally ascribed to 'P' (e.g. Gen. 5.1), and in the latter part of Isaiah. For the first object of creation LXX has 'thunder', which affords a good parallel with **wind**, but it seems not to have any support within the Hebrew tradition, and MT **mountains** should be retained. More difficult is the following phrase, translated by NRSV as **reveals his thoughts to mortals**. This is unexpected, both in the sense that it seems inappropriate in context, and also because of the textual difficulties that are raised. The word *śēḥō* is found only here in the Hebrew Bible; it presumably comes from an otherwise unattested root *śeaḥ*. The translation **his thoughts** is based simply on context; the antiquity of the problem is illustrated by the fact that LXX has 'Christon', seeing a form of the root *m-š-ḥ*. This 'messianic' interpretation seems not to have been taken up by any other translation. NEB offered a drastic modification of the Hebrew text to achieve the reading 'who showers abundant rain on the earth', but this is one of those places where REB has abandoned the conjectures of NEB and returned to the traditional understanding of the Hebrew.

The next phrase can be translated straightforwardly, as in NRSV, **makes the morning darkness**, but this seems a curious quality to attribute to God. It is also an odd contrast to the next doxological fragment, 5.8, where we have 'turns deep darkness into the morning'. An obvious) possibility is to suppose that a conjunction has dropped out, so that we should read 'morning and darkness' (BHS notes that some Hebrew manuscripts have the conjunction, and Barthélemy 1992: 657 offers a long list of translations and commentaries that have taken this option). The concluding line is best seen as a refrain. **The Lord is his name** is found three times in slightly variant forms in the 'Song of the Sea', Exod. 15.1-21; it occurs again, as we have seen, in the other doxological fragments in Amos, and seems to have been characteristic of hymns praising God as creator.

5.1-17. This section has often been regarded as one of the least organized in the book. It contains a variety of material, including another of the three hymnic passages of the kind we have just noted at 4.13, and a wide-ranging collection of oracular material. This has often led commentators on the book to suppose that this section was the end-process of accumulation through a series of redactions. A very different approach has been put forward by Bovati and Meynet (1994a), who see 5.1-17 as being the nucleus of an elaborate structure that takes in the whole book of Amos. It will not be possible here to explore this kind of rhetorical criticism in detail, but its existence should be noted as offering a different literary approach to Amos from that which has become conventional among English- and German-speaking scholars. (For those who wish to see the results of their approach in less technical form, Bovati and Meynet 1994b is an outline application of their approach in a well-known paperback series.)

5.1-2. The introduction here is similar to those found in 3.1 and 4.1, the main difference being that here the **word** is identified as a **lamentation**, a *qinah*. This is a standard designation of poems of mourning, the best-known example probably being David's lament over Saul and Jonathan (2 Sam. 1.18-25), described as a *qināh* in its introduction, v. 17. It is conventional to state that the *qināh* is characterized by a 3+2 metre, and that this gives a halting rhythm appropriate for the mournful nature of such poems. That may be true here, but elsewhere (not least in the lament in 2 Sam. 1) it is very difficult to claim that this is a feature of the whole poem, and it seems safer not to attribute a particular metrical structure to this kind of poem.

The *qināh* itself is found in v. 2. Israel, normally of course a masculine noun, is here described in feminine terms, as seems often to have been the case when Israel's helplessness and hopelessness are the basic themes. Elsewhere, particularly in Hosea, references to a **maiden** who was **forsaken** would have strongly sexual connotations, but they do not seem to be present here. The language is rather that of mourning, and in that sense we have an appropriate sequel to the devastation described in ch. 4.

5.3. Though often linked by commentators with what precedes, this oracle seems to stand independently, with its own introduction. *ki*, **For**, both here and at the beginning of v. 4, might serve as a link, but can equally be taken in an asseverative sense, 'Surely'. The theme is a variant of that found in Deut. 28.25, maintaining the links with that chapter already noted at 4.9.

5.4-5. The assertion of the inevitable fate of Israel in 4.6–5.3 is bracketed in 4.4-5 and our present section by condemnation of worship at the 'wrong' sanctuaries. This gives support to the idea that at least part of the reason for the harshness of Amos was what was perceived to be wrong religious practice. The verb *dāraš*, **seek**, has strongly cultic associations, so that the requirement is here being laid down of the necessity of proper cultic worship. It will be important to bear this in mind when we come to the cultic condemnation in vv. 21-24. Here the true 'seeking' of Yahweh is contrasted with the inherently false seeking involved in worship at **Bethel** and **Gilgal**. Their fate is assured. It would be unwise to take **go into exile** literally. Its parallelism with **come to nothing**, and the more general point that this is poetry, suggest that this is simply the language of extreme punishment. An interesting link is provided with Hos. 4.15, where not only are the same two sanctuaries mentioned, but also the word *'awen*, **nothing**, is actually used as a mockery of the name of the sanctuary, there described as 'Beth-aven'.

In our passage, of course, **Beersheba** is also condemned. Many have seen this reference as a later elaboration added when the material was edited in Judaean circles; certainly it is striking that the prohibition of **crossing over to Beersheba** lacks any explanation, and it is noteworthy that LXX does not use the name here but simply renders the component elements of the word ('well of the oath'). On the other hand, this is not the only implicit condemnation of Beersheba in Amos (cf. 8.14), and it may well be that our passage serves as a warning that it is not only northern sanctuaries that are condemned. Any potential southern rivals to Jerusalem would be equally unacceptable.

5.6-7. The command of 5.4 is now repeated, but transformed from the direct divine command into third-person prophetic speech, with the consequences of failure set out. NRSV paragraphing is at this point rather regrettable, in that it destroys the chiasmus of the original. We should read vv. 4b-6a as a unit, with 'Seek' and 'live' as the outside members, enclosing references to 'Bethel' and 'Gilgal', and the warning not to 'cross over to Beersheba' as the central member of the unit. Not all the literary units of this kind detected by Bovati and Meynet (1994a) will be found persuasive, but what we have here does seem likely to be a deliberate use of chiasm.

The verb *ṣalaḥ* is somewhat unexpected, and many modifications have been proposed. (BHS lists three in its margin.) The difficulty is that the normal meaning, 'to be strong or effective', seems inappropriate. One possibility (BDB 852a) is to suppose that we have to do with a homonym, a second verb of identical spelling, meaning 'rush'; this would be the meaning here and in the descriptions in Judges 14–15 of the spirit rushing upon Samson. Most more recent lexicographers have felt that the evidence does not warrant the proposal of this distinct verb. NRSV **break out** appears to be a free rendering of the MT.

The **house of Joseph** is a common way of referring to the northern kingdom, Israel (cf. 1 Kgs 11.28). In LXX, which is followed by NEB but not REB, it is balanced by a reference to the 'house of Israel'. But MT **Bethel** should be retained, as it provides a further link with v. 5.

The imagery of **fire** recalls the destruction pictured in ch. 1, its potency here stressed by the warning that there will be **no one to quench it**.

Verse 7 is printed in NRSV as following directly from v. 6, but this has been a minority opinion. Both NEB and REB have moved it so as to follow v. 9, and Crenshaw (1975: 124-25) lists many suggestions from older commentators on how this whole section should be divided. Certainly it is possible to see a link between vv. 7 and 10, with the doxological fragment in vv. 8-9 taken to be an insertion. But we need to remember that we have no knowledge of 'rules' that laid down how Hebrew poetry was to be constructed, and it therefore seems wise to accept the text as it has come down to us (there are no significant modifications of order among the ancient witnesses), and to see how that may best be understood.

A measure of interpretation is essential, since the Hebrew has nothing which corresponds to NRSV **Ah**. Perhaps a stronger interjection would be appropriate, bringing this verse into line with 5.18 and 6.1 ('Alas for...'). However these difficulties are resolved, the theme is the familiar one of lack of respect for **justice** and **righteousness**. The verb *hāpak*, **turn**, can be taken more or less literally as in the proverbial saying in 2 Kgs 21.13, where it refers to the turning over of a dish, or metaphorically in the sense of 'overturn'. The use of the verb here is surely deliberate; not only does it provide a link back to 4.11, but it is found again in v. 8, with Yahweh as the subject. Indeed, LXX has transformed the sense of this verse, assimilating it to the following hymnic fragment and making the deeds here described Yahweh's own.

5.8-9. Here we reach the second of the three hymnic passages discussed at 4.13. As we have already noted the order of verses and the connections of thought in this part of the book are far from clear; certainly the hymn seems very intrusive in its present position. Once again the theme is of Yahweh as creator, and it is now generally agreed that a translation along the lines of NRSV is appropriate. *kīmah ukᵉsīl* are linked both here and in Job (9.9; 38.31), and the reference to **Pleiades and Orion** is widely accepted. We cannot be certain whether such references indicate an interest in and a knowledge of astronomical matters within Israel, or whether we should rather see a literary borrowing based ultimately on Mesopotamian sources.

One proposal which seems to have been abandoned by most modern translations is that allusions to constellations are also to be found in v. 9. Thus the NEB translation of the relevant part of the verse was:

who makes Taurus rise after Capella
and Taurus set hard on the rising of the Vintager.

This proposal had been made by Driver 1953, and the influence of Sir
Godfrey Driver in the translation of disputed passages in the NEB is
well known. To make best sense it also required the modification of
verse order noted above. Such a reading is described by Barthélemy
(1992: 662) as 'seductive', but is not accepted. Strikingly, REB, while
retaining the modified verse-order, has reverted to the traditional understanding of the verse. This seems wise, not least because three textual
emendations are needed to obtain the reference to constellations, in
addition to the need to propose an unusual meaning for the verb *bālag*.
Its normal sense 'be cheerful' is not close to what is required. This is
admittedly a problem for any translation, as we shall see below.

Consideration of v. 9, then, will be in its MT context. Before we reach
it we note the use in v. 8 of *ṣālmāwet*, **deep darkness**, best known for
its occurrence in Ps. 23.4, and for the traditional translation there,
'shadow of death'. In the present context there seems no doubt that the
reference to darkness is appropriate. God's control can extend to the
reversal of the normal order of darkness and light.

Less certain is the weight to be given to the following references to
the waters of the sea. That too may refer to Yahweh's control of even
apparently hostile elements. A reference to tidal activity is possible,
though there is little else in the Hebrew Bible that would support such
an understanding. Should we perhaps see an allusion to Noah's flood?

One unexpected feature of v. 9, whether or not one accepts the astronomical interpretation, is the repetition of one of the key words. *šōd*,
destruction, occurs twice, and though one can envisage repetition for
emphasis, it is not a characteristic feature of Hebrew poetry and must
be somewhat suspect here. We have already noted the problem of the
verb *bālag*; NRSV has **flash out**, which again seems remote from the
basic meaning. Hammershaimb (1970: 81) claimed to be able to detect
as that basic meaning the sense 'to shine' and that to let devastation
shine over fortresses meant their destruction. It is an ingenious but perhaps not wholly persuasive proposal.

5.10-13. We are back in the situation envisaged by v. 7, of those who
lacked respect for justice. Here the *mōkiah* is the arbitrator or judge, the
one who reproves in the gate, the traditional place for the maintenance
of community law. What is different from v. 7 is the use here of the
third person plural. The earlier verse was in the second person, and that

is found again in v. 11, which may suggest that some expansion of the original has taken place. Care must be taken, however, with suggestions like this; the way in which they are sometimes expressed appears to envisage that those responsible for the expansion simply failed to notice the grammatical form of the basic text. So it is at least as plausible to see the switch to the second person as a deliberate device to heighten the tension of the attack.

'Attack' is certainly the right way in which to describe v. 11. It is clear that the behaviour described in the first part of the verse is regarded as unacceptable, though it is not easy precisely to define it. NRSV **trample** appears to be based on an emendation, recommended also by BHS, reading *buskem* for the difficult MT *bōšaskem*. It is not clear whether REB accepts MT, treating the form either as a loan-word from Akkadian with the meaning 'levy taxes', or whether it achieves that meaning through emendation of the improbable Hebrew to some form of *š-b-s*. The parallel with **levies of grain** gives some support to the REB understanding.

When we come to the second part of the verse, however, we must be careful not to be too readily swept away by the vigour of the attack. Clines (1995) does not use this text as an example of his 'Meta-commentary', but it would serve his purpose well. The text makes it sound as if to **have built houses of hewn stone** and **planted pleasant vineyards** is itself a matter for condemnation. In fact it is difficult to envisage how the people would have survived had there not been such houses and vineyards. Here they serve simply as the occasion for a further almost gloating assertion that those condemned will reap no benefit from their efforts.

ki at the beginning of v. 12 is perhaps best taken as asseverative, 'Surely I know' (thus Wolff), though NRSV's understanding, that it offers a reason for the judgment announced in the previous verse, is also possible. Where NRSV does not quite bring out the appropriate nuance is in the use of **righteous**, which in modern English has a strongly religious connotation. Here the sense of *ṣaddīq* is much more likely to be 'innocent'. The context is legal, and REB 'bully the innocent' achieves the required sense. Those who are actually innocent are treated as guilty; bribery is endemic; and where justice should be dispensed, **in the gate** (cf. v. 10), those too **needy** to have an eloquent advocate will be **pushed aside**. Some will ask how much things have changed in many societies over the better part of 3000 years.

Verse 13 reads curiously, as if proposing that discretion is the better part of valour, not an attitude characteristic of our poet. It is widely seen as an interpolation (Soggin 1987: 92). In its present context it may denote that the author had less confidence than is suggested elsewhere that all evil really would be punished.

5.14-15. Both the theme and the language used to express it are reminiscent of vv. 4 and 6. Though there is no specific reference to Bethel, the link with the earlier passages seems to suggest that Bethel is now regarded as inherently **evil**. The possibility should be borne in mind that the rather prosaic form of 14b is an implied quotation of the liturgy of the people's worship. They regularly claimed that the LORD was with them; this might become true if they were indeed, improbably in the poet's view, to **seek good and not evil**.

The linkage of the language of the law and of worship continues in v. 15, where it is stressed that the demand to **love good** is bound up with the need to **establish justice in the gate**, the context of the fierce condemnations in the preceding verses. The rest of the verse may be anticipatory, speaking as if the threats so commonly expressed in this book have already been carried out, or it may be that some disaster had already taken place from which a **remnant** had survived. Here as most usually in the prophetic literature, 'remnant' simply means 'survivors'. It appears to be quite free of the theological weight that has come to be added to it, of a 'saved' or even 'saving' remnant.

5.16-17. *lākēn*, **therefore**, appears to act as a purely formal link; there is nothing in what has preceded of which the picture of disaster here portrayed can be regarded as the consequence. Its solemnity can be measured by the threefold use of the divine speaker: **the Lord** (*yhwh*), **the God of hosts**, **the lord** (*ᵃdonai*). This and many comparable passages throughout the book remind us that these are not merely Amos's own words, as suggested by 1.1; the author/editor is regularly taken to have access to the words of God himself.

These words encompass the whole community, beginning with the places where they would most likely be found (**squares and streets**). The **wailing** implies formal mourning ceremonies, such as would have begun with **Alas! alas!** Two further terms for **mourning** and **wailing** are used in 16b, thus illustrating the importance of the place of laments in ancient Israel, as in many other traditional societies. The paucity of terms available in our modern usage is illustrated by the fact that NRSV, like other versions, has to use 'wailing' for both *misped* and *nehi*.

Curiously, in v. 17 *misped* repeats the usage of 16a, the first word translated 'wailing' in NRSV. Some (cf. BHS) have seen this as evidence of a secondary addition; alternatively it might function as an inclusio, balancing the whole unit. NRSV follows BHS and many commentators in supposing that the preposition *'el* has been misplaced; the Hebrew text would read '(call) wailing to those skilled in lamentation'; the minor emendation makes much better sense. There is some versional support (notably the Peshitta) for the change, but it is more likely that the editors there were 'improving' the sense rather than preserving an otherwise unattested original.

5.18-20. The condemnation now becomes more specific, and this has given rise to one of the most debated passages in the whole book. It begins with a subtle irony, juxtaposing the funeral language of *hoi* (**Alas**) with the eager anticipation of *hammit'awwīm*, where NRSV **desire** is perhaps barely strong enough: 'long for'. It is clear that the object of their longing, **the day of the LORD**, is popularly regarded as a triumphant occasion of some kind, but there has been much debate about more precise understanding, not least because of the great interest in eschatological texts, of which this had been widely held to be one of the earliest examples. (Barstad 1984: 89-110 offers a full discussion of the use of the term throughout the prophetic literature, with a very helpful short outline of the scholarly views that were current when he was writing.)

As well as the possible eschatological implications of the term, two explanations have dominated much recent discussion of 'day of the Lord' language. One, associated particularly with von Rad, has seen links with the theme of holy war. In fact von Rad's own setting out of this link was a good deal more nuanced than one might suppose from statements of his views by others, but he does acknowledge that 'Amos's contemporaries (may have) cherished the expectation of such an uprising to war and victory on the part of Jahweh' (von Rad 1965: 124). The second explanation has been to emphasize the cultic associations of the 'day of Yahweh', often with a reference to Ps. 118.24. This link was developed particularly by Mowinckel. He modified his views as to the nature of this link, but remained convinced that 'when misfortune befell the people, hope was linked with Yahweh's new "day" in the festival' (Mowinckel 1956: 142; a footnote refers to Amos 5.18).

Each of these explanations has come under critical scrutiny in recent years, and the reasons for this are well summarized by Barstad. In addition to more detailed points he notes our uncertainty whether 'holy war' really was an ancient theme in Israel, and our lack of precise knowledge about a plausible cultic context. An important positive point which he makes, and one that ties in well with the concerns of the present commentary, is to stress the need to see the overall prophetic context of 'day of the Lord' language (Barstad 1984: 93-97). At the beginning of our reading of Amos we noticed significant links with Joel. These have been less prominent since the opening chapter, but here they emerge again very strongly. The 'day of the Lord' is a key theme in Joel, and its portrayal has much in common with what we find here. In both collections it is set out in strongly negative terms (cf. e.g. Joel 1.11). The particular expression of that negative perception both here and in Joel is as darkness (Joel 2.2; 2.30-31 [MT 3.3-4]). There is one contrast that in fact only serves to strengthen the link. In Joel the imminence of the day of the Lord was seen as occasion for public lament (Joel 1.14-15); here, by contrast, it is eagerly desired, and an important part of the prophetic message is to warn against such mis-placed hopes. We may notice also that a further transformation of the motif occurs in the next unit in the Book of the Twelve (Obad. 15), but that is beyond our present concerns.

Reverting now to our own text, the impact of the day is compared with the danger inherent in an encounter with **a lion** or **a bear.** The use of these two creatures for unwelcome situations in proverbial form (Prov. 28.15) may suggest links between our poet and the wisdom tradi-tion. Verse 20 rounds the unit off by bringing out once again the theme and language of v. 18.

5.21-24. Whether or not the famous condemnation of cultic practice which follows was originally intended to follow directly on 5.18-20, it must certainly now be read in that context. There is no ambiguity in the way in which the poet has Yahweh reject that practice. **Hate** and **despise** are both very strong verbs, leaving no doubt as to the depth of the rejection. More difficult to determine is the force of the suffixes. In the MT four of the words describing the various religious ceremonies (**festivals, solemn assemblies, grain offerings** and **offerings of well-being of your fatted animals** [this last being just two words in Hebrew]) have the second person suffix *-kem*, **your**, and it would be possible to argue that the condemnation is of these ceremonies as offered by the specific group to whom the text was addressed, rather than as a more general rejection of religious rites. On the other hand '*ōlōt*, **burnt offerings**, does not have a suffix, and in any case the terms used are very general; the '*aṣārāh*, for example, was any kind of 'solemn assembly'.

Discussion of this passage, and of comparable material elsewhere in the Latter Prophets (Isa. 1.10-17; Hos. 6.6; Mic. 6.6-8 are probably the best known passages) has been so extensive that it is impossible to summarize it here. Part of the difficulty these passages have caused arises from the fact that much detailed study of the Prophets has been undertaken by those with a specific religious interest to maintain, so that the possibility that God does not approve of religious practice is an extremely destabilizing one. Even so, it is unexpected to find texts of this kind esteemed and handed down in a community whose very *raison d'etre* seems to have been correct religious observance, and it implies an ability to hold together potentially conflicting views of religious commitment. It is not appropriate here to enter into detailed discussion of the work of Hanson and others in tracing divisions within the Second Temple community, but if the book of Amos reached its final form in that context, then that is the setting against which this attack should be seen. Hanson (1979: 179) does in fact recognize our passage as illustrative of 'a long history of tension between prophet and temple cult'. As noted in the Introduction, Thompson (1999: 69) resolves the problem by postulating the Hellenistic period as the most likely time of origin of passages like this, but that seems an improbably late date.

The particular construction of v. 22 is unclear. The introductory *ki 'im* could be understood as either concessive ('although') or as conditional ('if'). NRSV favours the concessive understanding but obscures the fact that the Hebrew has no balancing clause, since the phrase 'Even though...burnt-offerings' stands alone in the Hebrew, not linked to what follows as in NRSV and NEB. It has been widely held that some disruption has taken place here, but there is no agreement as to its form.

A curious by-way of translation that seems now to have been abandoned is the suggestion in NEB that the **fatted animals** were actually 'buffaloes'. Whether such creatures existed in Palestine is doubtful; certainly they formed no regular part of any known sacrificial rites.

At v. 23 the form changes to prohibition. If God's rejection of sacrificial worship in the preceding verses would have seemed strange to all but some modern Liberal Protestants, divine dislike of music is even more unexpected. Clearly it is the whole cultic complex that is here being rejected. One curiosity is obscured by the fact that modern

English no longer distinguishes between singular and plural 'you'. Whereas in vv. 21-22 those being condemned were addressed in the plural, here the **your** is singular ('thy songs...viols' in AV). Though BHS proposes an emendation to a plural form, all the versional evidence supports the singular, which should be retained, even though we can no longer know who was being condemned so specifically.

Finally we reach the positive requirement against which the preceding condemnations are to be set. Its allegedly revolutionary nature has sometimes been exaggerated, as if there were other individuals or groups who rejected **justice** and **righteousness**. In fact such qualities were universally acclaimed, if less often achieved. Nevertheless it remains true that this stress is one of the distinctive features of the Prophets, and is a recurrent motif in the Book of the Twelve (cf. Hos. 6.6; Mic. 6.8). Perhaps one particular element that we may overlook is the concern that it should be reliable. An **everflowing stream** is one that can be relied on to provide water at all times and was not merely a seasonal wadi. Similarly justice and righteousness were to be permanent characteristics.

5.25-27. These three verses in prose are still concerned with worship and offerings, but apart from that general theme they have few obvious links with what has preceded. BHS speculates that much of the material may be later glosses, and Hammershaimb is not alone among commentators in describing this section as 'among the most difficult in the whole book' (Hammershaimb 1970: 91). The question in v. 25 appears as if it is expecting the answer 'No', but such an answer would of course be in flat contradiction of the Pentateuchal tradition, much of which is devoted to spelling out the essential nature of **sacrifices and offerings**, and setting them within the wilderness period.

Various proposals have been made to avoid this apparent contradiction. Van der Woude (1982: 41-42), for example, claimed that the verse 'must be combined with verse 26 for grammatical reasons. The interrogative *ha* governs two co-ordinate clauses, so that...we have to render the two verses: "When you brought me sacrifices and offerings those forty years in the wilderness, O house of Israel, did you take up Sakkuth...?"' He goes on to claim that the text 'actually presupposes' that sacrifices were brought in the wilderness. It might be so; but such an understanding goes against both the natural reading of our verse and a lengthy and virtually unanimous tradition of interpretation.

The natural understanding of the passage would be to see it as aimed at answering a natural concern expressed following the destruction of the temple by the Babylonians. While many will have felt that this destroyed the whole basis of their religious practice, one possible response would have been the argument that the ritual practices could not claim such status as had been commonly assumed. Such an approach could be traced here, in the broadly similar passage Jer. 7.21-22, and in such a passage as Isa. 66.1-2, which appears to be opposed to the reconstruction of a temple. The understanding reflected in the anti-temple speech of Stephen in Acts 7.42-43 embodies the same tradition.

The reference in Acts makes use of the LXX of Amos, which in v. 26 departs a long way from MT. Instead of the admittedly very cryptic Hebrew reference to **your king**, LXX took it to refer to 'Moloch', so that in Acts we have 'the tent of Moloch, and the star of your god Rephan'. The place of deposition has also been modified; where MT threatens with **exile beyond Damascus**, LXX, looking back on the Babylonian conquest, and treating prophetic words as foretelling the future, saw here removal 'beyond Babylon'. This is comparable with the LXX reference to Assyria that we noted at 3.9.

Barstad (1984: 120-22) offers a useful survey of the very varied understandings of v. 26 found in the ancient versions, noting that whereas most modern translations (not NEB/REB) and commentators have seen in **Sakkuth** and **Kaiwan** the names of gods wrongly wor-shipped by the people, the versions by and large did not understand the reference in this way. It is noteworthy that these are the forms offered in NRSV, though the actual Hebrew words are *sikkut* and *kiyyun*. It is widely accepted that the words have been deliberately mis-vocalized in the Masoretic rendering, so as to link them with various forms of abomination.

Barstad's conclusion is that we do not have enough evidence to be confident of proposing a 'correct' interpretation, and that we can only say that there is condemnation here of some form of non-Yahwistic worship, and that the gods referred to were in some sense planetary, a link between Kaiwan and Saturn being the clearest evidence of this. If, as we have suggested elsewhere, our text is best understood as being brought together in the Second Temple period, then some knowledge of Babylonian planetary worship would be the more understandable.

It is noteworthy that most modern translations speak of the threatened divine punishment in terms of **exile**. To what extent such a notion is already present in the original text is difficult to say, but modern inter-

preters have detected here the theological associations found in the
notion of 'exile' which would not be so apparent if a word like 'deportation' were used.

6.1-3. Another lament introduced by *hoi* follows; we may compare
5.18, though there the following participle was linked with second person pronouns. If there have been implications in the earlier part of the
book that Jerusalem might consider itself exempt from the harsh judgments passed upon Bethel and other places, any such illusions are now
put right. The inhabitants of **Zion** and of **Mt Samaria** are under equal
condemnation. As with much of the material from the Second Temple
period, this appears to reflect the bitterness of an excluded group
against those who are **at ease** and **feel secure**, that is, presumably, the
ruling groups in the community, pictured somewhat ironically as **the
notables of the first of the nations**. The last line of v. 1 is so vapid as
to be virtually meaningless, but the various proposals to modify it tell
more of the ingenuity of scholars than of their ability to convince.

A comparison then follows. **Calneh** and nearby **Hamath** were in
Syria, well to the north of Israel; **Gath** was one of the constituents of
the **Philistine** pentapolis in the South-west. Calneh and Hamath are
referred to also, the former under the slightly variant spelling 'Calno',
in Isa. 10.9. Strikingly the context there is also a comparison with
Jerusalem and Samaria. It seems as if these cities had become, as it
were, catchwords, used as a warning against the complacency of Israel,
which was no **better than these kingdoms**. NRSV offers **you** (in the
text) and 'they' (in the margin) as alternatives; the person is not made
clear in MT, though BHS proposes modifying the text to make a second
person reading specific. If adopted that would ease the transition to the
second person in v. 3, though others have taken that as in effect an
independent oracle. In it we note a link back to 5.25, where the same
verb (*nāgaš*), there translated simply 'bring', was used. There the
'bringing' had been 'sacrifices and offerings'; here it is **a reign of violence**, with the implication that the two were essentially similar. The
remainder of the verse also seems to refer back to what has preceded,
for **the evil day** must surely be a reference to the day of the Lord. It
may be that NRSV **put far away** does not quite convey the intended
sense, which seems to suppose that the day is in fact far away.

6.4-7. Another lament introduced by *hoi*. The contents of this passage
provided Clines with some rich material for his 'metacommentary' on
the book (Clines 1995: 78-84), though perhaps the most vivid of his

insights derive from the way in which other commentators on the book
have supposed that everything condemned in Amos must betray signs
of inherent wickedness, rather than from the text itself.

Certainly it would be unwise to press too closely all the details of
Amos's condemnation. **Ivory** seems to have been a particular cause of
irritation to our poet (cf. 3.15). It may have symbolized luxury. Ahab,
we recall, had an 'ivory house' (1 Kgs 22.39), and anything associated
with Ahab implied condemnation. Ezekiel 27.6, 15 also include ivory in
the description of the luxuries associated with Tyre. In a similar way
the verb *sarah*, to sprawl or over-hang, is used here and in v. 7 (NRSV
lounge) in a derogatory way. The actions described in this section are
not wrong in themselves. After all, even the rich have to sleep, to eat
and drink, and may perhaps be allowed a little music and the keeping
up of outward appearances. No doubt, as with the ivory decorating the
beds, there will have been an element of luxury in what is described;
not many could afford to eat **lambs** or **calves**, and the drinking took
places from *mizraqim*, large **bowls** or even vats. But all these inherently
neutral actions are described in hostile terms, so that everything done
by those of whom the poet disapproves is regarded with displeasure.

More difficult to decide is the point raised by Barstad, who devotes a
whole chapter to 'the *mrzh* institution' (Barstad 1984: 127-42). The
word left untranslated occurs in v. 7, and is rendered as **revelry** in
NRSV. The only other occurrence of the term is at Jer. 16.5, and at first
glance that seems to conflict with our passage, for NRSV there has
'house of mourning'. But it is well-known that the barriers between
mourning and festivity may soon break down. The term occurs in several other ancient Near Eastern texts, and Barstad concludes that the
overall reference is to a sacred meal, possibly in a funerary context.

Two possibilities, which are not necessarily mutually exclusive,
emerge for the understanding of our passage. It might be that the
excesses associated with the *marzēah* were the cause of the condemnation here, that what had begun as a religious rite had degenerated into
debauchery. This would fit in well with the view that a main thrust of
our book is the condemnation of false religious practice. But it would
also be possible to suppose that the funerary character of the occasion
offered an ironic message. What had started as lavish festivity would
soon be seen as a funeral, with the revellers **the first to go into exile**.

One curiosity remains; the reference to **David** in v. 5. Many have
seen it as a later gloss, allegedly on the ground that it overloads the

metre, but also, one suspects, because it is somewhat embarrassing in context, associating David with those here being condemned. It might be a later addition, from a period when David was regarded as the patron, or even the inventor (the force of **improvise** here), of song, but it could equally reflect suspicion of the temple and its worship, in which the Psalms of David will have played a prominent part. If Wolff (1977: 272) were right in translating the verb *pārat* here as 'howl', his other assertion, that the reference to David is a later gloss, becomes curious; would David have been regarded as 'howling'? In any case this passage offers a clear link with the assertion that God did not care for 'songs' and 'melody' at 5.23.

6.8. Yahweh is here pictured as delivering an oath, with a very solemn introduction; BHS regards the words bracketed by NRSV as an addition, but this is unnecessary. As at 5.16 we have an example of a strictly unnecessary repetition of the divine name for greater emphasis, and Barthélemy (1992: 669) justifies the retention of these words on the grounds of the great violence of the contents of the oath. Its precise thrust is, however, difficult to determine. In its other occurrence, in Ps. 119, the verb *tā'ab* means to 'long for'. That is quite inappropriate here, and versions and commentators have achieved the required sense, either by supposing that the pi'el form of the verb has the sense **abhor**, or that an emendation should be made to a form of *tā'ab*. Certainty here is impossible; we can note only that once again, as previously in this chapter, it seems that we have a hostile reference to Jerusalem, **the city**.

6.9-10. This prose section is linked to what has preceded by its concern with mourning, and may be seen as part of the judgment. Verse 10 is particularly difficult in detail, though its overall sense is clear. The *dōd*, NRSV **relative**, is normally the paternal uncle, but that makes poor sense in the context, seeming to imply that there was a member of the family whose duties were to act as an undertaker! Both BHS and *DCH* II, 423 propose an emendation linking the beginning of the verse with v. 9, and claiming the support of LXX. This would yield 'but a few shall remain'. But this does not really help with the interpretation of the remainder of the verse, and it may be better to retain MT. Soggin (1987: 107-108) has a useful discussion, and concludes by suggesting that the reference is to 'an epidemic explained as a divine punishment'. The last part of the verse seems to reflect the kind of superstitious belief not altogether extinct today. **We must not mention the name of the LORD**; implying that if we keep quiet he may forget all about us.

6.11-14. This somewhat fragmentary section begins with another assertion of total disaster, afflicting great and small alike. It leads on into a pair of rhetorical questions of the kind sometimes found in the wisdom literature. This was described by Wolff (1977: 284) as 'a sapiential device', characteristic of the wisdom literature. We have already noted a more extended series of such questions in 3.3-8. But whereas in that earlier series the expected answer was 'Yes, of course', here the implied answer is the reverse, 'Certainly not'.

This is clear enough with the first question, **Do horses run on rocks?**, the rocks in questions being 'crags', quite unsuited to horses. It is well-known that in its MT form the second question works quite differently, 'Does one plough with oxen?', to which the answer is of course Yes. A minor textual change, involving no consonantal change but reading *babbāqār yam* for MT *bab^eqārīm*, was apparently first proposed by the eighteenth-century German scholar J.D. Michaelis, and is now accepted by most modern translations: **Does one plough the sea with oxen?** We should most probably accept this change, even though the present form of MT is certainly ancient; it is already found in LXX, and Barthélemy (1992: 672) feels that the second comparison, which seems natural enough to a modern reader, would not have made sense in the world of Amos. Barthélemy therefore proposes retaining MT and seeing the second question as an explanation of the first, in terms of the folly of the people.

In any case the people's behaviour is treated as an absurdity and is condemned in terms very similar to those found at 5.7. It is linked in a way which seems to require another 'Woe' to a condemnation of the people's falsely based confidence. NRSV text and margin express the two possible interpretations of v. 13. The text treats **Lo-debar** and **Karnaim** as place-names. They are known as such from other references, and it is possible that events in those places, of which we know nothing, had been treated as a sign of divine favour. But if there is a reference to the place-names it is not a random choice. A different way of interpreting the names is offered in the margin: 'A thing of nothingness' and 'Horns'. Their rejoicing is over the merest trivia; their supposition that they had gained victories '**by our own strength**' is false confidence. (We may note that NEB/REB favour this reading in the text, with a marginal reference to the place-names.)

The word *ki* with which v. 14 begins is taken by NRSV, surely rightly, as asseverative, **Indeed**. It introduces an assertion of impending doom over the whole land from **Lebo-hamath**, in the North, down to **the Wadi Arabah**, which ran into the Dead Sea in the South. An interesting comparison can be made with 2 Kgs 14.25, according to which the prophet Jonah had announced that this same area would be brought under Israelite control. That hopeful prophecy is here as it were annulled. This is important in reading the Book of the Twelve. The inadequacies of Jonah as a prophet will be drawn out in that part of the larger book that is named for him, and readers are alerted here to the danger of simply following Jonah.

7.1-3. This is the first in a series of visions found in the latter part of the book, and regarded by many scholars as one of the closest links with the prophet Amos himself. There is inadequate evidence for judgments of this kind; the importance of vision as a means of communication with the divine will is basic in much of the prophetic tradition, and on into the biblical and postbiblical apocalypses. All we can say is that the visions seem to relate to the quite widespread literary tradition of the chosen servant being admitted into the divine council, to learn what is in store for the community. We should note also that the importance given to the visions is not easily compatible with the widely-held view of the prophet as preacher; we should not reduce these visions to sermon illustrations.

Form-critically this and the next vision in 7.4-6 may be described as 'event visions', but this is scarcely more than a surface analysis of the material. The introduction to these two, together with those in 7.7-9 and 8.1-3, is identical. Only the fifth vision (9.1) has a different form. Very striking is the use of the first-person singular pronouns in the visions. Earlier in the book 'I' and 'me' had normally been put into the mouth of God himself. Here the words spoken are ascribed to the prophetic figure. This is a literary device; it would be unwise to take it as a guarantee of 'genuine' personal experience.

Whether it was **the Lord God** himself who was **forming locusts** is not clear. That is one reading of the Hebrew, but the sense 'someone was forming' is equally possible. It might seem as if the reference to locusts offers a link back to the early verses of Joel, but in fact the word here used, *gobi*, is not one of those found in Joel. Its only other occurrence is at Nah. 3.17. The last few words of the verse are regarded as a likely gloss by BHS and are put in brackets by NRSV, but we should regard them as an integral part of the text. There may be an element of explanation of the time of year at which the swarm took place, but it is also significant that at this stage the king is not affected. The prerogative of **the king's mowings** has been completed. When we read the verse in its total context, however, we shall soon discover that the king will not remain unscathed for long (v. 11).

Most of the major religious figures in the Hebrew Bible are pictured from time to time as intercessors, and Amos is no exception, though as with other figures we shall see that this role is eventually abandoned. The locust swarm is seen as a threat to **Jacob**, pictured as too **small** to be oppressed in such a way. The prophetic perception of the nation's inadequacy offers an interesting contrast with its self-perceived 'strength' in 6.13. In this first vision the intercession is held to be successful: **It shall not be**. We are clearly not intended to see this as a 'false prophecy', announcing something that did not in fact take place and thereby falling foul of the criteria laid down in Deuteronomy (18.21-22), but it is not easy to discern objective grounds on which this can be seen as different.

7.4-6. A second vision follows, virtually identical in form with the first. The main difficulty is textual. The natural translation of MT *lārib bā'ēš* would be 'to contend with fire', which scarcely yields acceptable sense. A host of suggested emendations is listed by Barthélemy (1992: 675-76), but they have to be conjectural. The proposal in BHS, *lahebet 'eš*, giving the sense of ' a flaming fire' seems too far from MT to be plausible, and more likely is the suggestion of Hillers (1964), taken up by several recent commentators, requiring much less drastic consonantal change, to read *lir^ebīb 'eš*, 'a rain of fire'. This would accord well with the cosmic sense of **the great deep**; increasingly in the visions we move from the kind of unfortunate happening that might be regarded as among the ordinary mishaps of life to matters of universal concern. **The land** is more literally 'the portion' (*ḥeleq*) and it is possible that this alludes to Israel as 'God's portion'. This seems to be implied by LXX, and would fit well with Deut. 32.9, where Jacob is described as 'the Lord's own portion'. In vv. 5 and 6 there are only two minor changes from the equivalent development of the first vision. The first is the use of a different verb, *ḥādal*, **cease**, which to modern Christian readers will seem less 'theological' than the 'forgive' of v. 2, but that may not be inherent in the usage. Secondly, the addition of **also** emphasizes that the visions are to be read as part of a series.

7.7-8. The third vision produces problems of rather a different kind, problems that are bound up with the history of interpretation. The introduction is very close to that found in vv. 1 and 4, but there is no need to follow the recommendation of BHS, based on LXX, and make the form identical. Minor variations of this kind seem typical of Hebrew literary style. The extent of this unit is also unclear. NRSV follows the custom of most English translations in setting out v. 9 as part of what has preceded, but it is only loosely related to the vision. In the present form of the text, v. 9 seems to function as an elaboration of the vision whose primary function is to act as an introduction to vv. 10-17 (Ackroyd 1987: 196).

Within the vision, the chief difficulty concerns the details of the **wall**. The traditional interpretation, still followed by NRSV, is that the otherwise unknown word *'anāk* means a **plumbline**. Many a sermon must have preached calling for 'straightness' in the hearers, using the analogy of Amos's plumbline. The supposition is that the basic meaning of the word is 'lead', so that the meaning of 'a wall of lead' would be 'a wall built with a plumbline', the weight of lead being appropriate for such a use (Auld 1986: 19). Auld goes on to point out that many modern scholars have questioned this meaning, and since he wrote, a whole book has been devoted to this question: Beyerlin 1988. In it Beyerlin maintains that the meaning of *'anāk* is not 'lead' but 'tin'. The word is not otherwise known in Hebrew, but the view held by Beyerlin and others is that our word is cognate with Akkadian *annaku*, meaning 'tin'. The difficulty then becomes that of visualizing a tin wall, and Hoffmeier (1998: 309) quotes a distinguished Assyriologist who says 'I have not the faintest understanding of the sense of the passage'!

If the reading 'tin' is correct, we may note first of all that we are concerned with a vision, and it is not necessarily the case that what is seen in vision corresponds with empirical reality. Certainly the reflective brightness associated with tin lends itself well to a visionary context. Less certain must be the view that tin symbolizes military might, and that we have here a picture of a people with a sense of false security behind the defence of their city wall. Despite parallels cited by Beyerlin, such a wall seems very difficult to envisage. In any case the important point is that the *'anāk* is held in Yahweh's hand, and portends a threat to the people. This conclusion has led Williamson to the view that the traditional understanding of the vision, involving a plumbline, can still be maintained. No ancient Israelite plumblines have survived, but perhaps they were partially made of tin (Williamson 1990: 112).

However that may be, the outcome is clearly enough expressed in
v. 8b. With this vision there is no suggestion of intercession, but here,
and in the next vision at 8.2, we have only Yahweh's verdict. The people are here named **Israel**, as against the 'Jacob' for whom the intercession had been made (vv. 2, 5), but there is no obvious reason for
supposing that this in itself has negative connotations. The exact force
here of the common verb √'-b-r is not clear. NRSV **pass by** offers a neutral form, whereas REB, with 'pardon', is more interpretive. A likely
proposal is that of Wolff (1979: 301), who suggests that 'pass by' here
has the sense of overlooking wrong doing. Yahweh had done that in
response to intercession in vv. 3, 6; he will do so no more.

7.9. This verse, as noted already, seems to have little direct connection with the vision, whereas the reference to **Isaac** at once provides a
link with what follows (v. 16). There are no other references to **the
high places of Isaac**, so we cannot know whether a particular place
was envisaged. Possibly Beersheba, mentioned elsewhere in Amos (5.5;
8.14) and associated with Isaac in Genesis (26.33), is intended. This
assumes that the reference is to the ancestor named in Genesis, though
the spelling of the Hebrew form of the name here (*yiśḥaq*) differs from
that in Genesis (*yiṣḥaq*); the difference may be merely orthographic.

The last two lines of v. 9 contain the kind of wordplay favoured in
Hebrew poetry but impossible to bring across in translation. The word
ḥereb has two senses, 'lay waste' and 'sword', and both are used here.
A better-known wordplay is found in the next of the visions, at 8.1-2.

The section ends with a reference to Jeroboam, and this provides an
important link to the prose passage which follows. 'Historical' readings
of Amos have seen **the house of Jeroboam** as a reference to Jeroboam
II, who was apparently the ruler of Israel through much of the first half
of the eighth century BCE (2 Kgs 14.23-29), and certainly it would be
possible to envisage God's rising **with the sword** as an allusion to the
fate of Jeroboam's son Zechariah (2 Kgs 15.8-12).

The more usual reference to 'the house of Jeroboam', however, has
Jeroboam I in mind (e.g. 1 Kgs 12.34, and frequently thereafter in
Kings), and in view of the links with 1 Kings 13 displayed in the next
section of Amos, that, rather than a specific reference to a 'Jeroboam
II', may be what is intended here. We should understand 'the house of
Jeroboam' as epitomizing the whole governing structure of Israel.

7.10-17. This much discussed passage has often been held to provide
the basis for our knowledge of the 'historical Amos'. It is assumed that

we have a genuine fragment of prophetic 'biography', perhaps associated with Amos's call to be a prophet. On such a reading he was called from his traditional task as a **herdsman and a dresser of sycamore trees** around his home in Judah to go to the Northern Kingdom and utter words of warning there. His threats were seen as a conspiracy and **Amaziah, the priest of Bethel**, acting as the king's representative, warned Amos to return to his homeland.

It is a possible reading, but one that is much less securely based than its widespread and often unquestioning adoption warrants. The fact that it is not easy to envisage circumstances in which such a biographical fragment would have been handed down may not be too serious an objection, given that we know very little of the transmission of such material in ancient Israel. Gevaryahu was one of the first recent scholars to raise questions about the reliability of traditions of this kind. His proposal was that the story arose from a combination of oral tradition and 'research on the text itself', and was not to be dated significantly earlier than the final time of composition of the book (Gevaryahu 1975: 43). The difficulty here is that we know very little about what such 'oral tradition' meant in practice. Melugin has also drawn attention to the way in which what becomes accessible to us here is a reflection of the power and interests of the story-teller rather than a making available to us of neutral historical information. The quotations are scarcely likely to be a verbatim record; rather 'an author might have employed well-known conventions of prophetic speech to lend verisimilitude to the plot which the composer chose' (Melugin 1996: 76).

In fact there is an additional complication. Stories of the kind we have here are rare in the prophetic books. Ackroyd (1987: 195-96) has noted this, and then goes on to draw attention to the similarities between the language of this passage and that found in the books of Kings. In particular this leads us to consider the strikingly close resemblance between this story and that told in 1 Kings 13. There too a man of God, unnamed in 1 Kings, was sent by God from Judah to Bethel, the royal sanctuary that was under the patronage of a king called Jeroboam. There too unavailing threats were uttered against the man of God, before his return to Judah. The 1 Kings 13 story then develops in a way that has no parallel in Amos, but the links in the first part seem too close to be coincidental. They are supported by incidental points such as the unexplained reference to 'high places' in v. 9, found also at 1 Kgs 13.2.

The literary form of the two stories differs, however, in that the technique used here has no close parallel in 1 Kings. Here the description of the mission is put into the mouth of **Amaziah, the priest of Bethel**. It begins with a theme used throughout the ages by those in authority who sense themselves to be under threat: someone has **conspired**. The verb, *qāšar*, is found 13 times in Kings, and it is interesting that, together with its derivative noun *qešer* it is found five times in 2 Kings 15, which provides the background for this story.

Amaziah's words are seen to provide close links with v. 9, most obviously in the threat against **Jeroboam**, more generally in the way in which the devastation of v. 9 now becomes the announcement that **Israel must go into exile away from his land**.

No indication is given of the royal response to Amaziah's message, but the priest is next pictured as addressing Amos himself. Some have seen this in friendly terms, the intruder being advised to get away while the going was good. It is doubtful whether we are intended to read it in this light, and if it was so intended we can only say that Amos's reply was pretty ungracious. He is here described as a *ḥōzeh*, **seer**. This usage has been the basis for a variety of theories concerning the prophetic role, some seeing a North-South divide, others proposing developments in the perception of prophetism, away from purely visionary experiences to a deeper insight into the nature of the divine word. Attractive though such theories may be, one has to recognize that there is little evidence to support them. 1 Samuel 9.9 might lead us to expect that 'seer' (there *ro'eh*) was an obsolete title which needed explaining to later ages, but in fact the term *ḥōzeh* is most commonly used in the late books of Chronicles.

Another link with the story in 1 Kings 13 is provided by the command to **earn your bread** in Judah. It is not clear why NRSV has adopted this curious translation: RSV 'eat bread' is much more natural, and enables us to see the link with 1 Kgs 13.8-9, where the same phrase is used and plays a key role in the development of the story. Whether there is any link with the idea of a seer/prophet as needing payment for his work is less clear, and seems not to be the focus of attention here.

Anti-Bethel polemic is a theme found commonly in the books of Kings—not only in 1 Kings 13 but down to the story of Josiah's destruction of the altar and the high place (2 Kgs 23.15-18) which is anticipated at 13.2. Here the claims of Bethel are set out by Amaziah in what is surely intended by the compiler to be an ironic manner. His readers would have known that there could only be one place properly described as **the king's sanctuary** and **the temple of the kingdom**. That was Jerusalem. Amaziah was making false claims which would justify the fate about to be pronounced.

This brings us to the much-discussed v. 14. The Hebrew is deceptively simple, and could be literally rendered, 'No prophet I, and no son-of-a-prophet I, but a herdsman I and a dresser of sycamores'. English versions and commentaries have varied in their rendering. Some have taken this as a straight statement, dissociating the speaker from prophetic status; commentators might then speculate on the difference between Amos and the 'professional prophets', who are then pictured as a rather deplorable group. It seems certain that this additional speculation should be resisted; the idea of Amos as the 'gifted amateur' calls to mind Groucho Marx's reluctance to have an operation performed by a 'gifted amateur brain surgeon'. It may still be the case that the editor wished to differentiate between Amos and the normal perception of prophets.

A second view, very popular among English-speaking scholars, has been to maintain that the verbless Hebrew should be rendered by English past tenses, 'I was no prophet...' In the context of a historical reading this interpretation has certain clear advantages. It implies that, though Amos had not come to 'prophethood' by the normal means, whatever they may have been, he had received a direct call from God (v. 15), and that his claim to prophetic status was more valid than that of the ordinary run of prophets. This would tie in with positive references to prophets and prophecy elsewhere in the book (2.11; 3.7-8). Against it is the fact that despite the assertion to the contrary by Rowley, natural Hebrew usage would correspond to an English present text (Auld 1986: 26-27). (The reference to Rowley needs clarification. The view outlined in this paragraph, that the appropriate translation should be 'I was no prophet...', owed much to an article by Rowley, 'Was Amos a Nabi?' in the Festschrift for O. Eissfeldt, published at Halle in 1947. The original article was never, to the best of my knowledge, reissued in the English-speaking world, but Rowley summarized his argument in several of his books, e.g., Rowley 1946: 101-102.)

Other proposals have been made as to the best way to resolve the tension in this verse, such as the suggestion that it should be read in question form: Am not I a prophet? (Ackroyd 1987: 205). Again, we should note that the identical expression, *lō' nābī 'ānōkī*, 'I am no prophet', is

found at Zech. 13.5. Commentators on the Zechariah passage have
often speculated on the possibility that that is a quotation of Amos, but
it may be that the two passages should each be seen as a (?conven-
tional) disclaimer of prophetic status in the Second Temple community.

It will in any case be apparent that a different understanding becomes
appropriate if we are looking at this narrative as a story about the
eponymous hero of the book rather than as a first-hand memorial. In
that context we are being invited to reflect upon God's action in bringing down the Northern Kingdom, 'the house of Jeroboam', and that is
done by the retelling of a familiar story. Just as the version in 1 Kings
13 had been set at the beginning of that kingdom's separate existence in
the biblical picture of its history, so our version of the story is set in a
context that points to its precipitous collapse.

The other phrases in v. 14 also become less significant if the verse is
not regarded as an autobiographical fragment. *bōqer*, **herdsman**, is a
different word from that translated 'shepherds' in 1.1, and suggestions
of emendation in either direction should be resisted. Whereas in 1.1
claims concerning Amos's social standing might be detected, here we
have a word linked to the normal designation of cattle. The description
of Amos as **dresser of sycamore trees** is a curiosity, unexplained on
any reading. The trees concerned were probably mulberry figs; the
work involved in 'dressing' (?slitting) them was a very brief task,
undertaken normally by those of low social status, and in any case
confined to the Shephelah, some distance from any of the other areas
mentioned in the book. The Targum already sensed the difficulty, and
made Amos the owner of the trees, but no entirely satisfactory explanation has been proposed.

The prose section ends with the double affirmation that the prophet's
calling was truly of divine origin, an important claim in view of the
harsh oracle about to be credited to him. Earlier passages had mostly
been broad and unspecific in their denunciations; here we have a condemnation concerned with one individual and his family.

The word attributed to Amaziah in v. 16 offers an obvious link with
v. 9, which had warned of the destruction of Israel, set out in each verse
in parallel with Isaac. The verb *nātap*, here translated **preach**, more
literally means to 'drip'. It is several times used in the context of
prophetic oracles; whether some form of ecstatic utterance is envisaged
remains uncertain.

The fate of Amaziah and his unfortunate family is then announced.

The oracle is not couched in such a way as to imply any concern for, still less sympathy with, the **wife** and **sons and daughters** of Amaziah, but is rather concerned with the shame such happenings brought upon him (Sanderson 1992: 207). His wife becoming a prostitute would have been a special shame for Amaziah, for unions between priests and prostitutes were particularly condemned (Lev. 21.7, 14). The violent death of his children meant that there would be no posterity to preserve his line. The whole of this episode needs to be read in the context of a society where honour and shame were of very great importance.

This is relevant also when we are told of the loss of his **land**. Such a loss would also be shameful. The story of Naboth (1 Kgs 21) reminds us of the importance attached to the family land. God was regularly pictured as allotting ($\sqrt{h\text{-}l\text{-}q}$) the promised land to its intended owners; here the verb is used in a passive form to show the reversal of that situation. It is to be **parcelled out by line**. *ḥebel*, here translated 'line', was the plot of ground envisaged as the basis of the divine allocation. Instead of dying secure in the promised land, however, Amaziah was condemned to exile **in an unclean land**. The passage ends with the emphasis brought out by repetition: in the Hebrew the last line of v. 17 is identical with v. 11b. It is not clear why NRSV has changed 'must' to 'shall surely' and 'his' to 'its'.

8.1-3. After the narrative interlude the series of visions resumes. The basic structure of this fourth vision is similar to that of the third, in 7.7-9. Their formal identity is helpfully set out in tabular form by Soggin (1987: 118). In addition the questioning, **Amos, what do you see?** (cf. 7.8a), and the verdict, **I will never again pass them by** (cf. 7.8b) are identical with the earlier passage. The threatening nature of the two visions, unbroken by any suggestion of intercession, is also closely comparable.

Where this vision does differ from what has preceded is in its use of word-play. Amos is shown a *kᵉlūb qayiṣ*, literally 'a basket of summer'. The use of the word *qayiṣ* already provides a link with the warning of destruction in 3.15. It has been suggested that the fact that the fruit had been gathered and placed in a basket already suggests that it was no longer living fruit, but this may be over-fanciful. Such fruit was part of Ziba's gift to David at 2 Sam. 16.1, and there is no suggestion there of any special nuance being intended. What is clear is that the word *qayiṣ* is taken up in a word-play. Some scholars (e.g. Auld 1986: 18-19, following Gese) have held that the wordplay only reinforces the basic

meaning of the vision. We are to see in the gathering of the fruit suggestions of 'death the reaper'. As noted above, some will see this as an
over-reading of the text, but the threatening element remains. *qayiṣ*
means **the end**, and that is to be Israel's fate.

It may be appropriate to see the oracle in v. 3 as rounding off the
whole series of visions. (The fifth vision, beginning at 9.1, stands apart
in form from the preceding ones.) It is much disputed whether MT
songs (*šīrōt*) **of the palace** should be emended to *šarot* or some similar
form to give the meaning 'singing women' (regarded as probable by
BHS margin and thus NEB, following many commentators). Not dependent upon textual emendation is the understanding of the second noun,
heykāl, which could be taken either as 'palace' (NRSV margin.) or as
temple. Perhaps we need not commit ourselves to a specific meaning;
the point is the universality of **wailings**. Again, at the end of the verse,
the exact construction is not clear, but the general sense unmistakable.
The Hebrew seems simply to say 'they have cast out. Hush!', and it is
possible that some textual corruption has occurred. As in 6.10 the only
possibility is to **be silent**.

8.4-6. The introductory summons to **hear this** is reminiscent of the
earlier series of oracles, though the introduction there had the fuller
form 'hear this word' (3.1; 4.1, etc). The contents of this passage also
offer a link with earlier material, in this case ch. 2, especially vv. 6-8. In
particular the charge that those accused **trample on the needy, and
bring to ruin the poor of the land** is very close to 2.7, similar vocabulary being used in a different arrangement. Implicit here is the point
made explicit in 2.7, that the needy and the righteous can in effect be
identified.

Verse 5 lacks any close parallel in the earlier denunciation. Opinions
will differ whether the reference to **new moon** and **sabbath** here offers
any light on the early history of these occasions and the religious observance associated with them. The natural understanding of the verse
would suggest that the first part is concerned with insufficient reverence
for religious observances, whereas the latter part seems more concerned
with the kind of oppression involved in dishonest trading. Though the
traditional understanding, stressing the ethical rather than the religious
concerns of Amos, has tended to separate out these two areas, this may
be a false dichotomy. The practice of 'adjusting' the weights is condemned in the Torah (Lev. 19.35-36), and set there in the context of the
proper recognition of what the Lord had done for his people, and a

similar understanding may be appropriate here.

With v. 6 we return to the links with ch. 2, especially v. 6 there. In one sense the accusation is the exact opposite of the earlier one, for here the offence is to **buy the poor**, whereas in ch. 2 it was their sale that was condemned! But we should not make too much of this difference. The point is that it is wrong to envisage the poor as chattels which could be disposed of, bought or sold, simply as was convenient for the well-to-do. The end of the verse takes up again the theme of false trading, this time the practice of including the *mappal*, **the sweepings of the wheat**, in what was being sold.

8.7-8. This passage seems to stand independently. It consists of an announcement that Yahweh **has sworn** an oath, followed by a theophany of judgment. The oath is curious in that here God swears **by the pride of Jacob**, whereas in 6.8 he had abhorred the pride of Jacob. Is the expression here ironical? In fact the content of the oath itself is rather conventional when compared with the vigour of the denunciations found elsewhere in the book.

With v. 8 we return to a theme that runs through much of Amos: that of earthquake. Whereas at 1.1 it would be possible to understand this simply as a note of date, here it is made very clear that the earthquake is itself a manifestation of divine power, which brings humans to **mourn**. The second half of the verse is substantially identical with 9.5, and NRSV has made minor emendations to the Hebrew text to bring it into line with the later passage. (In its first occurrence the word translated **the Nile** is spelt unusually, and commentators are divided as to whether this is simply an alternative way of spelling a foreign name, or is a textual error. At 9.5, where virtually the same expression is found, the spelling is the conventional one. The issue is discussed by Barthélemy 1992: 684-86, with a lengthy treatment of mediaeval Jewish views.)

Another emendation to the usual form of the Hebrew text seems to be required toward the end of the verse. Whereas older translations had something similar to AV, 'it shall be cast out and drowned' the usual more modern custom is to follow the $q^e re$, reading $w^e ni\check{s}q'ah$ for $w^e ni\check{s}qah$, giving the sense **sink again**.

Regardless of the textual details, it is striking that the comparison, both here and at 9.5, is with the **Nile of Egypt**. There seems no particular reason for seeing a reference to the Exodus tradition; presumably the fluctuations of the Nile were widely regarded as a remarkable phenomenon.

8.9-10. The 'day of the Lord' theme is introduced once more. Here it is linked with a characteristic concern of the apocalyptic writings, the overthrow of the natural order (cf. Mt. 24.29). The sun is literally 'brought in' by God, as if being brought back to its own dwelling-place. The consequence of all this reflects the overturning of the popular expectation of the day of the Lord already noted at 5.18. God will **turn** (*hāpak*, a very frequent word in this book; this is its fifth occurrence) their joyful expectations into **mourning**.

8.11-12. Another threat is introduced, though its content proves to be somewhat different in kind. Its opening is identical with 9.13, but we shall see, when we come to that verse, how very different the consequences are there envisaged to be. What is unexpected in our present context is that **famine** is on this occasion not to be taken literally. It is almost as if the threats that run through so much of the book are here being 'spiritualized', so that the deprivation of the divine word is now a more serious matter than lack of food and drink. Whatever may be the case earlier in the book, here we are confronted with the priorities of a religious group.

This is brought out still more markedly in the following verse, where the religious group is anxiously seeking **the word of the LORD** in vain. We need not worry about the lack of geographical awareness apparently shown by the balance of **north** and **east**; Hebrew was less precise about compass-points than most moderns.

8.13-14. But whatever v. 11 may have said we are not to forget that the inevitable punishment will bring about literal **thirst**. The reference to **beautiful young women** is curious; the book has shown few previous signs of partiality to feminine charms. It is perhaps their vulnerability that is implied here.

The particular focus of condemnation is unusual in Amos. For the most part the offences condemned have been what we should describe as ethical or more specifically 'social', as in the earlier part of this chapter (8.4-6). Here, however, it seems as if idolatry is in mind, and this is an important part of Barstad's case in maintaining that the basic polemics of the book are religious (Barstad 1984: 143-201). He notes that to **swear by** a God normally implies the worship of that God, and that is the natural understanding of this passage.

We know nothing of an **Ashimah of Samaria**, and various proposals have been made. It could imply 'guilt', in accordance with the normal meaning of the word as a common noun. If that were so, two obvious possibilities present themselves. If we suppose that Amos is to be read in conjunction with the books of Kings, the reference could be to the golden calves set up by Jeroboam at Bethel and Dan (1 Kgs 12.28-30), the particular concern here, in the light of ch. 7, being that at Bethel. Such a reading might be supported by the mention of Dan in the next phrase of our verse, but it is not obvious why such an oblique form of reference should be used. If the condemnation is really of Bethel why not say so? Such reasons lead Barstad (1984: 163) to regard such an interpretation as no more than 'unfounded guesswork'. Alternatively, we could translate by some such expression as 'the wicked deed of Samaria' (so *DCH* I, 417a), and in that case the reference could be less to false religious practice than to the wrongfulness implicit in the very existence of the northern kingdom.

The remainder of the verse, however, makes it more probable that we should see here a reference to a divine being. Perhaps there is a link with another piece of religious polemic: 2 Kgs 17.30, which also refers to an 'Ashima', the word spelt slightly differently but the reference probably identical. It is possible also that reference to 'Eshem-Bethel' in the texts from the Jewish colony at Elephantine provides a further link, though there is no agreement as to the interpretation of that phrase (Porten 1968: 174-76). (The emendation to 'Asherah' proposed from time to time and suggested by BHS, seems less likely.) Most probably we should see a reference to a local manifestation of the worship of a goddess with a widespread cult in the ancient Near East, best seen here as part of the polemic against Samaria already noted in chs. 3–4. It is of at least incidental interest that such polemic is one of the themes that may hold together on the one hand the rivalry between Northern and Southern kingdoms in the eighth century and earlier, and on the other that tension between Jerusalem and Samaria under Persian rule that is a basic concern of the book of Nehemiah.

The other references seem clearer. The **god** of **Dan** is best understood as an allusion to the images set up there by Jeroboam (1 Kgs 12), though there are few other references to Dan. Much important archaeological work has taken place at the site, and Goulder proposed that some of the Psalms originated in the cult there. He found support for this in the similarity between the expression here, **as your god lives**, and similar phraseology applied to Yahweh in the Psalms (Goulder 1982: 29).

We have already noted opposition to **Beersheba** by the redactors of our book (5.5). If the book reached its final shape in the Second Temple period, we may detect here opposition to any shrine that might be seen as a rival to Jerusalem, particularly if, as is implicit here, it was a place of pilgrimage (**the way**). Despite the powerful arguments of Barstad (1984: 193-99), this seems a more likely understanding of the passage than his proposed detection of a link between this text and a possible Ugaritic reference to a deity *drk*. Just as in 5.2 Israel was pictured as fallen with no hope of rising again, so here more specifically that fate would befall sanctuaries regarded as alien. It remains uncertain whether the places condemned in this verse were in some way associated with one another, or are simply representative of such alien places of worship.

9.1. Another vision follows, though its form is significantly different from those we have considered in chs. 7 and 8. The extent of this passage is not clear, and though its general picture of devastation is obvious enough, difficulties arise when we try to become more specific. It is not clear, for example, whether there is any basic difference between a vision of destruction such as we find here, and the numerous oracles announcing destruction that we have encountered earlier in the book. Auld, following Gese, argues strongly that this vision is properly to be seen as the climax to the others in the series, 'like the experience of waking out of a dream' (Auld 1986: 22). Other scholars have been much more sceptical, stressing the differences between this and what has preceded, and seeing the present passage as a later addition (Soggin 1987: 121-22).

Our main concern, however, is with the book as we now have it, and there is no dispute that this vision forms an integral part of that. There is no reference here to the prophet being shown anything; instead he sees **the Lord standing beside the altar**. MT *'al mammizbeaḥ* might more naturally be translated 'above' or 'upon' the altar, and that might be more appropriate as a picture of judgment. Many have supposed that the altar in question would have been that at Bethel, taking the prose narrative in 7.10-17 as providing the context for the visions, but it is at least arguable that this should be seen as a condemnation of all unacceptable cult practice. Any such altar would then be condemned.

It is not clear by whom the work of destruction is to be accomplished. MT, followed by NRSV, has a command to the prophet to **Strike the capitals**, but BHS margin proposes as a probable reading, supported by many commentators, that this action was undertaken by God himself.

Thus Soggin (1987: 119), 'I will shatter violently the capitals...' The word translated 'capital', found several times in the description of the lampstand in Exodus 25, is *kaptor*. It is risky to find wordplays where none are intended, but it is noteworthy that this not very common word is used again, apparently in quite a different sense, as a place-name, in v. 7. Is it too fanciful to see the Philistines, mentioned there, as playing a part in the pictured destruction?

The devastation, which begins with the altar, passes out through the **thresholds** and leads into the destruction of **all the people**. Though the general sense here is clear enough, the Hebrew construction is difficult. NRSV **shatter** implies that this is still part of what is required of the prophet, but an emendation to a first person singular is widely accepted, making the action even more specifically that of God himself. Soggin's rendering 'all will perish in the earthquake' is valuable in placing this vision within the context of the whole book, but, as he himself recognizes, 'to say the least this is doubtful' (Soggin 1987: 120). Though certainty is impossible it is clear overall that the threat moves from the overthrow of buildings to the complete destruction of the people so that **not one of them shall flee away** or **escape**.

9.2-4. To where might they hope to escape? One obvious possibility would be **Sheol**, the place of the dead, clearly pictured here as being below the surface of the earth, but there is no hiding-place there. As in Ps. 139.8 neither Sheol nor **heaven** would provide a place of escape. ('Heaven' here may be a misleading translation if readers envisage it as in the Christian tradition, a place of bliss for the faithful dead; 'the sky' is in effect what is meant.) The following lines picture other possible hiding-places, though no translation can bring out the assonance of the Hebrew with its succession of *cha* sounds. In any case, all possible hiding-places are equally useless. One might think of a mountain-top as a curious place to **hide**, but **Carmel** was regarded as particularly inaccessible (cf. 1.2). The **sea-serpent** here is not an alien creature but part of Yahweh's creation which will carry out divine instructions (cf. Ps. 104.26). Elsewhere (e.g. 4.3; 6.7), being carried **into captivity** by **their enemies** had been seen as itself a devastating punishment; now that is too good for them, and they are doomed to additional punishments. In this harrowing context, the last line seems almost to be meant ironically—it is certainly an understatement!

9.5-6. The last of the doxologies (cf. 4.13; 5.8-9) follows. A feature that unites all three passages as a kind of refrain is **the LORD is his**

name. This passage differs from the previous two in its reference to God at the very outset, **The LORD, God of hosts**, and many have supposed this to be a later addition to give added solemnity (cf. BHS margin). There can be no certainty on that point, but the Psalm-like material that follows is reminiscent of the earlier passages. There are affirmations of divine power in participial form (relative clauses **who...** in English). The theophany itself is reminiscent of Ps. 104.32 for the idea that it only needs God to **touch the earth** for disastrous consequences to follow. The translation **melts** for *tāmōg* both here and at Ps. 46.6 (MT 46.7) is traditional, but the sense may rather be 'totter'. The verb *'ab^elū*, here translated **mourn**, is the same as that found in 1.2 (NRSV 'wither'). Both this link, and the similarities between the remainder of 9.5 and 8.8b, and between 9.6b^a and 5.8b^a should warn us against dividing the different elements of the book too sharply from one another. Indeed the use of earthquake language here, together with the two links with 1.2 that we have just noted in these verses, hint at a broad *inclusio* binding the whole book together.

Verse 6 sets out a claim for the universality of the power of Yahweh. The language used is mostly familiar, the main difficulty occurring with the word *'aguddāto*, the root of which means 'bind'. NRSV **vault** is favoured by Crenshaw (1975: 72), where various other possibilities are considered.

9.7-8a. One might have expected that the proclamation of divine power would form an appropriate climax but the editors cannot forebear one more dig at the aspirations of the **people of Israel**. The **Ethiopians** (Heb. *kušiyim*) were black Africans, people on the very edge of Israel's ordinary experience, and thus, it might have been assumed, far beyond the concerns of Israel's own God. Not so; the two groups are here pictured as being of equivalent concern. The obvious tension with 3.2 ('You only have I known') is limited by the fact that both passages speak of the destruction of Israel. In any case, as we noted in the discussion of the earlier passage, it is unwise to treat poetry as a vehicle of precise information.

The remainder of the section shifts to speaking of Israel in the third person, but the thrust is the same. It begins with the standard affirmation of Yahweh's role in bringing **Israel up from the land of Egypt**, but then shifts to an assertion that two of the people's traditional enemies have equally been the subject of their God's concern. The **Philistines** are famously pictured as enemies of Saul and David in 1 Samuel;

it is difficult to be certain whether the reference here is to be associated with some actual experience or, perhaps more probably, is an allusion to those traditions. **Caphtor** is traditionally Crete, but there is little other evidence to link the Philistines with Crete, and we have noted already that 'Caphtor' was used in the vision of destruction in v. 1.

Kir also offers a link back to an earlier part of the book; at 1.5 it was asserted that the **Aramaeans** would be exiled to Kir. Here it is stated that that is their place of origin. The actual area envisaged is uncertain: somewhere in the eastern desert fringes. The literary linkage seems more important than any geographical identification. The passage reaches a climax in 8a, with its emphasis on the **sinful** state of **the kingdom** and the threat of destruction.

9. 8b. The great transformation in the nature of the book's message here takes place. Conventional historical approaches to Amos have found this to be a major problem, since it seems to contradict all that has gone before. The usual 'solution' has been to suppose that the main threat of destruction consisted of the words of Amos himself, and that this addition was the work of a later redactor. Perhaps such a redactor observed that Judah had not been destroyed, and felt that the original words must be qualified to take account of that fact (thus Mays 1969: 160).

The difficulty with views of this kind is twofold. First, it postulates an extremely literal-minded redactor, who is on the one hand convinced of the lasting validity of Amos's words and wishes to pass them on, yet who also has no scruple in modifying them in the most thoroughgoing way. Secondly, it supposes that **the house of Jacob** can refer here to a surviving Judah, whereas earlier in the book it has clearly been applied to those being condemned (3.13).

A literary rather than a historical resolution of the tension seems to be called for. It would be unwise to make a straightforward comparison between the end of Amos and the 'deus ex machina' resorted to by Greek playwrights, but the effect is comparable. The editor of the book is inviting us to see another dimension in the divine–human relation. The at times extremely unpleasant portrayal of God and his actions found in the earlier chapters is now claimed not to be the whole story; there is a forgiving aspect of the divine character that must also be taken into account.

9.9-10. For the moment, however, there are more words of threat. The verb *nūaʿ*, **shake**, is a favourite in the book of Amos, and here it is used in two quite different senses. First, to 'cause to wander' **among all the nations,** that is, the threat of deportation; then secondly, and more conventionally, 'shake' as **with a sieve.** The point of this simile is not altogether clear. One might expect that the unwanted rubbish would fall through the sieve, but here it seems more likely that it is retained in the sieve, so that Israel would be like the **pebble** held up in the sieve and ready for dumping. Nowhere else in the Hebrew Bible is this simile used in such a way. Verse 10 retains the overall note of threat, directed this time against those complacent enough to suppose that **evil shall not overtake or meet us,** but we are alerted to another dimension of the portrayal by the reference to *'ammi,* **my people. Sinners** though they are, they are nevertheless God's people. Will they be those upon whom 'the end' has come (8.2), or will they be those who receive God's prophetic words (7.15)? The basic threat of the book thus far leads us to suppose the former answer to be right, but the last few verses show a dramatic change.

9.11-12. Verse 8b had already given a hint that the threats which have dominated so much of the book might not be the whole story; the remaining verses of the book offer a dramatic transformation. More than a century ago Wellhausen is said to have characterized 9.11-15 as 'Roses and lavender instead of blood and iron'. It is an interesting reflection, both upon Wellhausen himself and upon many commentators who have followed him, that blood and iron should apparently be regarded as preferable to roses and lavender.

A historical reading virtually requires that this material should be seen as a secondary addition. That **the booth of David is fallen** must surely allude to the exile, the **booth** itself being either the whole city of Jerusalem or its sacred precincts. The last part of v. 11 would then clearly refer to the restoration of Jerusalem at the beginning of the Second Temple period. The promise that the people will **possess the remnant of Edom** also makes good sense in such a context. Hostility against Edom is characteristic of several passages from that time, such as Ps. 137.7 and Obadiah.

Reference to Obadiah may, however, alert us to a different way of reading these closing verses of Amos. Obadiah is the next component of the 'Book of the Twelve', and just as in the early part of Amos we noted links with the preceding book, Joel, so here it seems proper to see a link with the immediately following book—Obadiah, which begins with the words of 'the Lord God concerning Edom'. Interestingly ambiguous, too, is the reference to **nations who are called by my name**. This can be a way of referring to conquered peoples (cf. 2 Sam. 12.28), but it also may quite legitimately be read with universalistic overtones—a claim is being made for the widespread extension of the power of Yahweh.

We should also be aware of a different tradition of interpretation of 9.11-12, one which is found in the New Testament. The passage is quoted by James at Acts 15.16-17 in the setting of the 'Apostolic Council' said to have been held at Jerusalem to consider the position of Gentile believers in the early Christian church. Such a reading can only in the broadest sense be described as 'messianic', but the use of the passage in the Dead Sea Scrolls shows that the Judaism of the turn of the eras was looking for the 'fulfilment' of these words. Thus the Florilegium 4Q174 refers to 'the Branch of David who shall arise with the Interpreter of the Law [to rule] in Zion [at the end] of time. As it is written, 'I will raise up the tent of David that is fallen' (available in many collections of Qumran texts, but here quoted from Vanderkam 1994: 52). It is not appropriate here to look in detail at the nature of messianic expectation in later Judaism, but the importance of our text should certainly be recognized.

9.13-15. The book ends with an oracle which has attracted much attention among those who claim to be able to detect 'end-time prophecies' in the Christian Old Testament. A popular reading in such quarters has been to see this as pointing forward to the establishment of the modern state of Israel, which has been perceived as **rebuilding ruined cities**, and making the land fertile in the way pictured in v. 14. This commentary is being written as a new millennium draws near, and many have convinced themselves that this and comparable passages elsewhere in the Prophets will find some kind of 'fulfilment' in that time. This commentary is written from a very different world-view, and the suggestion made here is that we are in the presence of the kind of apocalyptic imagery reminiscent of such a passage as Isaiah 25, where again extraordinary fertility is envisaged. Any temptation in the well-fed West to denigrate such modes of expression needs to bear in mind how close to famine and drought ancient Israel often was.

At a literary and religious level this passage seems to function in a way closely comparable to the last verses of Hosea (14.4-8) and a section in Joel which we have already considered (3.18 [MT 4.18]). After many threats and warnings, in each book there is transformation to a promise of an idyllic future, in which the curse of the ground spelt out in Gen. 3.17 is done away with, so that the soil produces miraculously with little need for human effort.

The supposition that this passage reflects a 'postexilic' situation would be strengthened still more if one were able to accept the traditional translation of 14a, *wᵉšibtī et-šᵉbat 'ammi yiṣra'el*, 'I will bring again the captivity of my people of Israel' (thus AV). Modern versions are however surely right to offer a more general rendering such as NRSV, **I will restore the fortunes of my people Israel**. Whatever the historical setting, it seems legitimate to see two important links here. First, within the book of Amos itself, we have the same verb, *šub*, which was used in a threatening way in the oracles against the nations, 1.3–2.16, NRSV 'I will not revoke the punishment'. Now the verb is used in a very different sense. Secondly, the same phrase as is found here is employed in Joel 3.1 (MT 4.1), to remind us of the basic thrust of the Book of the Twelve toward restoration of the proper relation between God and people. Like the great majority of the prophetic collections (Isaiah is a notable exception), our unit of the larger Book ends on a confident note.

BIBLIOGRAPHY

What follows aims to provide fuller information about works cited in the commentary. It is not intended as a guide to further reading, though it is hoped that most of what would be found in such a guide is included here. A valuable bibliographical resource is provided by H.O. Thompson 1997, which lists 1729 items relating to Amos, together with a number of dissertations. Unhappily Thompson died before he could complete the final correction of his work, and it does contain a number of minor errors (e.g. the work of Coote 1981 is listed twice), and the indexes have a number of omissions and errors.

Ackroyd, P.R.
    1987   'A Judgment Narrative between Kings and Chronicles? An Approach to
                Amos 7.9-17', in his *Studies in the Religious Tradition of the Old
                Testament* (London: SCM Press, 1987): 196-208. Previously published in
                G.W. Coats and B.O. Long (eds.), *Canon and Authority: Essays in Old
                Testament Religion and Theology* (Philadelphia: Fortress Press, 1977).
Andersen, F.I., and D.N. Freedman
    1989   *Amos* (AB, 24a; New York: Doubleday, 1989).
Auld, A.G.
    1983   'Prophets through the Looking Glass: Between Writings and Moses',
                JSOT 27 (1983): 3-23.
    1986   *Amos* (OTG; Sheffield: JSOT Press).
Barstad, H.M.
    1984   *The Religious Polemics of Amos* (VTSup, 39; Leiden: E.J. Brill).
Barthélemy, D.
    1992   *Critique textuelle de l'Ancien Testament*. III. *Ézéchiel, Daniel et les 12
                Prophètes* (OBO, 50.3; Fribourg, Suisse: Editions Universitaires;
                Göttingen: Vandenhoeck & Ruprecht).
Bartlett, J.R.
    1973   'The Moabites and Edomites', in D.J. Wiseman (ed.), *Peoples of Old
                Testament Times* (Oxford: Clarendon Press): 229-58.
Barton, J.
    1980   *Amos's Oracles against the Nations* (SOTSMS, 6; Cambridge:
                Cambridge University Press)
    1986   *Oracles of God* (London: Darton, Longman & Todd).
Beyerlin, W.
    1988   *Bleilot, Brecheisen oder was sonst? Revision einer Amos-Vision* (OBO,

81; Freiburg Schweiz: Universitätsverlag; Göttingen: Vandenhoeck & Ruprecht).

Blenkinsopp, J.
1996   *A History of Prophecy in Israel* (2nd rev. and enlarged edn.; Louisville, KY: Westminster/John Knox Press).

Bovati, P., and R. Meynet,
1994a   *Le livre du prophète Amos* (Rhétorique Biblique, 2; Paris: Cerf).
1994b   *La fin d'Israël: Paroles d'Amos* (Lire la Bible, 101; Paris: Cerf).

Brueggemann,W.
1965   'Amos IV 4-13 and Israel's Covenant Worship', *VT* 15.1: 1-15.

Carroll R., M.D.
1992   *Contexts for Amos: Prophetic Poetics in Latin American Perspective* (JSOTSup, 132; Sheffield: JSOT Press, 1992).
1995   'Reflecting on War and Utopia in the Book of Amos: The Relevance of a Literary Reading of the Prophetic Text for Central America', in M. Daniel Carroll R., David J.A. Clines and Philip R. Davies (eds.), *The Bible in Human Society: Essays in Honour of John Rogerson* (JSOTSup, 200; Sheffield: Sheffield Academic Press): 105-21.

Clements, R.E.
1975   *Prophecy and Tradition* (Growing Points in Theology; Oxford: Basil Blackwell).

Clines, D.J.A.
1995   'Metacommentating Amos', in his *Interested Parties: The Ideology of Writers and Readers of the Hebrew Bible* (JSOTSup, 205; Sheffield: Sheffield Academic Press): 76-93. (This essay has appeared elsewhere in slightly variant forms.)

Coggins, R.J.
1995   'What does 'Deuteronomistic' mean?', in J. Davies, G. Harvey, and W.G.E. Watson (eds.), *Words Remembered, Texts Renewed: Essays in Honour of John F.A. Sawyer* (JSOTSup, 195; Sheffield: Sheffield Academic Press): 135-48.

Coote, R.B.
1981   *Amos among the Prophets: Composition and Theology* (Philadelphia: Fortress Press).

Crenshaw, J.L.
1975   *Hymnic Affirmation of Divine Justice: The Doxologies of Amos and Related Texts in the Old Testament* (SBLDS, 24; Missoula, MT: Scholars Press).

Cripps, R.S.
1955   *A Critical & Exegetical Commentary on the Book of Amos* (London: SPCK, 2nd edn).

Driver, G.R.
1953   'Two Astronomical Passages in the Old Testament', *JTS* NS 4.2: 208-12.

Gevaryahu, H.M.I.
1975,   'Biblical Colophons: A Source for the "Biography" of Authors, Texts and Books', in *Congress Volume Edinburgh* (VTSup, 28; Leiden: E.J. Brill): 42-59.

Gottwald, N.K.
1980   *The Tribes of Israel* (London: SCM Press).
Goulder, M.D.
1982   *The Psalms of the Sons of Korah* (JSOTSup, 20; Sheffield; JSOT Press).
Hammershaimb, E.
1970   *The Book of Amos: A Commentary* (Oxford: Basil Blackwell).
Hanson, P.D.
1979   *The Dawn of Apocalyptic* (Philadelphia: Fortress Press, 2nd edn).
Hillers, D.R.
1964   'Amos 7.4 and Ancient Parallels', *CBQ* 26: 221-25.
Hoffmeier, J.K.
1998   'Once again the "Plumb Line" Vision of Amos 7.7-9: An Interpretive
            Clue from Egypt?', in M. Lubetski, C. Gottlieb and S. Keller (eds.),
            *Boundaries of the Ancient Near Eastern World: A Tribute to Cyrus H.
            Gordon* (JSOTSup, 273; Sheffield: Sheffield Academic Press): 304-19.
Holladay, W.L.
1971   *A Concise Hebrew and Aramaic Lexicon of the Old Testament* (Leiden:
            E.J. Brill).
Hubbard, D.A.
1989   *Joel and Amos* (TOTC; Leicester: IVP).
James, F.
1939   *Personalities of the Old Testament* (New York: Charles Scribner & Sons).
King, P.J.
1988   *Amos, Hosea, Micah: an Archaeological Commentary* (Philadelphia:
            Westminster Press).
Koch, K.
1982   *The Prophets*. I. *The Assyrian Period* (ET M. Kohl; London: SCM Press).
Mays, J.L.
1969   *Amos* (OTL; London: SCM Press).
McKeating, H.
1971   *The Books of Amos, Hosea and Micah* (Cambridge Bible Commentary on
            the New English Bible; Cambridge: Cambridge University Press).
Melugin, R.F.
1996   'Prophetic Books and the Problem of Historical Reconstruction', in S.B.
            Reid (ed.), *Prophets and Paradigms: Essays in Honor of Gene M. Tucker*
            (JSOTSup, 229; Sheffield: Sheffield Academic Press): 63-78.
Meynet, R.
1998   *Rhetorical Analysis: An Introduction to Biblical Rhetoric* (JSOTSup, 256;
            Sheffield: Sheffield Academic Press, 1998).
Mowinckel, S.
1956   *He that cometh* (ET G.W. Anderson; Oxford: Basil Blackwell).
Murray, R.
1982   'Prophecy and the Cult', in R. Coggins, A. Phillips and M. Knibb (eds.),
            Israel's Prophetic Tradition: Essays in Honour of Peter R. Ackroyd
            (Cambridge: Cambridge University Press): 200-16.
Nogalski, J.D.
1993a   *Literary Precursors to the Book of the Twelve* (BZAW, 217; Berlin: W.
            de Gruyter).

1993b   *Redactional Processes in the Book of the Twelve* (BZAW, 218; Berlin:
               W. de Gruyter).
Paul, S.M.
1971   'Amos 1,3–2,3: A Concatenous Literary Pattern', *JBL* 90: 397-403.
1991   *A Commentary on the Book of Amos* (Hermeneia; Minneapolis: Fortress
               Press).
Polley, M.E.
1989   *Amos and the Davidic Empire: A Socio-Historical Approach* (New York:
               Oxford University Press).
Porten, B.
1968   *Archives from Elephantine* (Berkeley: University of California Press).
Rad, G. von
1965   *Old Testament Theology. II. The Theology of Israel's Prophetic
               Traditions* (ET D.M.G. Stalker; Edinburgh: Oliver & Boyd).
Rowley, H.H.
1946   *The Re-Discovery of the Old Testament* (London: James Clarke).
Sanderson, J.E.
1992   'Amos', in C.A. Newsom and S.H. Ringe (eds.), *The Women's Bible
               Commentary* (London: SPCK): 205-209.
Soggin, J.A.
1987   *The Prophet Amos* (ET J. Bowden; London: SCM Press).
Swete, H.B.
1914   *Introduction to the Old Testament in Greek* (Cambridge: Cambridge
               University Press).
Thompson, H.O.
1997   *The Book of Amos: An Annotated Bibliography* (ATLA Bibliographies,
               No. 42; Lanham, MD; London: Scarecrow Press).
Thompson, T.L.
1999   *The Bible in History: How Writers Create a Past* (London: Jonathan
               Cape).
Vanderkam, J.C.
1994   *The Dead Sea Scrolls Today* (London: SPCK).
van der Woude, A.S.
1982   'Three Classical Prophets: Amos, Hosea, Micah', in R. Coggins, A.
               Phillips and M. Knibb (eds.), *Israel's Prophetic Tradition: Essays in
               Honour of Peter R. Ackroyd* (Cambridge: Cambridge University Press):
               32-57.
Waard, J. de
1977   'The Chiastic Structure of Amos 5: 1-17', *VT* 27.2: 170-77.
Watts, J.W., and P.R. House
1996   *Forming Prophetic Literature: Essays on Isaiah and the Twelve in Honor
               of John D.W. Watts* (JSOTSup, 235; Sheffield: Sheffield Academic
               Press).
Williamson, H.G.M.
1990   'The Prophet and the Plumb-line: a Redaction-critical Study of Amos vii',
               OTS 26: 101-21.
Wolfe, R.E.
1935   'The Editing of the Book of the Twelve', *ZAW* 53: 90-129.

Wolff, H.W.
  1974   *Hosea* (ET G. Stansell; Hermeneia; Philadelphia: Fortress Press).
  1979   *Joel and Amos* (ET W. Janzen, S.D. McBride, Jr and C.A. Muenchow; Hermeneia; Philadelphia: Fortress Press).
World's Classics Bible = *The Bible: Authorized King James Version* (ed. R. Carroll and S. Prickett; The World's Classics; Oxford: Oxford University Press, 1997).

INDEX OF PASSAGES CITED

INDEX OF AUTHORS